Box 25

Box 25

Archival Secrets, Caribbean Workers, and the Panama Canal

Julie Greene

The University of North Carolina Press CHAPEL HILL

Set in Merope Basic by Westchester Publishing Services

Manufactured in the United States of America

Library of Congress Cataloging-in-Publication Data

Names: Greene, Julie, 1956– author.

Title: Box 25 : archival secrets, Caribbean workers, and the Panama Canal /
Julie Greene.

Other titles: Box twenty-five

Description: Chapel Hill : The University of North Carolina Press, [2025] |
Includes bibliographical references and index.

Identifiers: LCCN 2024029887 | ISBN 9781469679471 (cloth) | ISBN 9781469679488
(paperback) | ISBN 9781469679495 (epub) | ISBN 9781469682235 (pdf)

Subjects: LCSH: Foreign workers—Panama—History—20th century. | Foreign
workers—West Indies—History—20th century. | Black people—Panama—
History—20th century. | Panama Canal (Panama)—History—20th century. |
BISAC: SOCIAL SCIENCE / Ethnic Studies / Caribbean & Latin American
Studies | SOCIAL SCIENCE / Race & Ethnic Relations

Classification: LCC F1569.C2 G657 2025 | DDC 305.896/072870904—dc23/
eng/20240826

LC record available at https://lccn.loc.gov/2024029887

Cover art: Ship with Barbadians Arriving in Cristobal, Panama, 1909,
National Archives.

Portions of the introduction were previously published in a different form in
"Labor Migrants Who Changed the World," *Modern American History* 7, no. 1
(March 2024): 127–30 (published by Cambridge University Press). Portions of
chapter 4 were previously published in a different form in "Entangled in
Empires: British Antilles Migrations in the World of the Panama Canal,"
in *Crossing Empires: Taking U.S. History into Transimperial Terrain* (Durham, NC:
Duke University Press, 2020), 222–40. All material republished by permission
of the publishers.

Dedicated to the memory of Constantine Parkinson
and the many other Caribbean men and women
who built the Panama Canal

Who dug the Canal? Who suffered most, *even until now?* Who died most? Who but the West Indian negroes.

—JULES LECURRIEUX, Isthmian Historical Society Competition for the Best True Stories of Life and Work on the Isthmus of Panama, held in Box 25, Isthmian Historical Society, Canal Zone Library-Museum Panama Collection at the Library of Congress, Washington, DC

Contents

Illustrations

Box 25

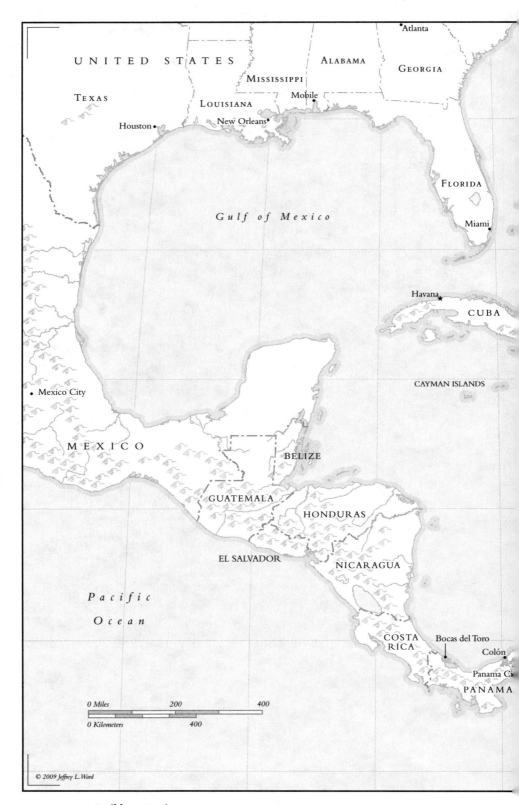

MAP 0.1 Caribbean Basin

THE CARIBBEAN BASIN

BAHAMAS

Atlantic

Ocean

TURKS AND CAICOS

DOMINICAN
REPUBLIC

Santiago de Cuba

HAITI

PUERTO
RICO

BRITISH
VIRGIN ISLANDS

Kingston

VIRGIN
ISLANDS

ANTIGUA AND
BARBUDA

JAMAICA

ST. KITTS AND NEVIS

MONTSERRAT

GUADELOUPE

Caribbean   Sea

DOMINICA

MARTINIQUE

ST. LUCIA

BARBADOS

NETHERLANDS
ANTILLES

ST. VINCENT AND
THE GRENADINES

ARUBA

Bridgetown

GRENADA

TRINIDAD
AND TOBAGO

V E N E Z U E L A

C O L O M B I A

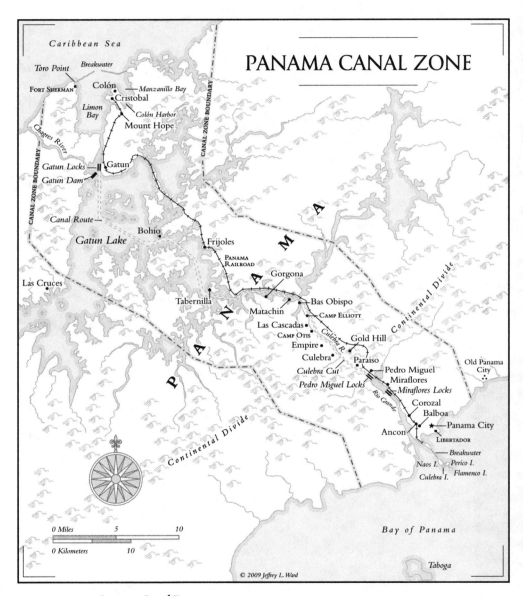

MAP 0.2 Panama Canal Zone

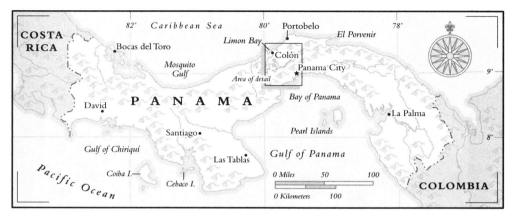

MAP 0.3 Panama

Introduction

A young man named Edgar Llewellyn Simmons sailed out of Carlisle Bay, Barbados, on a Royal Mail boat in January 1908 to work on the Panama Canal. After a two-week journey, he reached Colón and construction officials found him a place to sleep for the night. The whistle blew at 6:00 A.M. the next morning. When Simmons lined up, the boss picked every other man and gave each a pick and shovel. Simmons thought he would get a better job, since he'd not been chosen yet. Then came "one of our own West Indian fellow men" who took him to a dump car filled with coal, handed him a shovel, and told him to get to work unloading it all. The bosses called him "Shine."

So begins the story of Edgar Simmons, one of the tens of thousands of men and women who traveled to Panama during the construction decade from 1904 to 1914. They left homes in Barbados, Jamaica, St. Lucia, Antigua, the Bahamas, Grenada, and other Caribbean islands. Simmons's story is held in Box 25 of the Isthmian Historical Society Collection at the Library of Congress along with 111 other first-person testimonies by canal workers. The testimonies resulted from a competition in 1963 for the "Best True Stories of Life and Work" during the construction of the Panama Canal. The idea was to capture the experiences of that vast army of Afro-Caribbean laborers who, decades earlier, had built the spectacular Panama Canal. They constitute the best first-person accounts in existence by Afro-Caribbean workers, the true "canal builders" whose work reshaped the Western Hemisphere. The narratives tell dramatic stories of laboring on the canal project amid landslides, premature dynamite explosions, disease, and cruel bosses. For decades scholars and journalists have included anecdotes from the testimonies in their histories of the construction project. Yet they have never subjected the documents to in-depth analysis, to ask what we can learn by examining which individuals, out of the nearly 200,000 workers in the Canal Zone during the construction era, entered the competition. How did these workers choose what stories to tell, and how did their experiences compare to those of other men and women? What secrets are held inside Box 25?

Most of the hundreds of thousands of men and women who worked to build the Panama Canal were of African descent from across the Caribbean.[1] They dug, shoveled, dynamited, cooked and cleaned, and labored in the

FIGURE 0.1 Photo of Box 25, Isthmian Historical Society Competition, Canal Zone Library-Museum Panama Collection, Manuscript Division, Library of Congress

massive industrial sites as blacksmiths, carpenters, and machinists. In the early 1960s as the fiftieth anniversary of the Panama Canal's completion in 1914 approached, Ruth C. Stuhl, president of the Isthmian Historical Society, designed a competition open to all non-US employees. She wanted to capture the experiences of laborers from the British Caribbean. The historical society placed ads for the competition in newspapers in Panama, Jamaica, Barbados, British Honduras, Trinidad, Antigua, St. Vincent, St. Lucia, and Grenada, and sent notices about the competition in several thousand food packages distributed to disability relief recipients. The straightforward instructions declared that the historical society wanted to gather true stories of life and work on the Panama Canal during its construction. It noted that little had been written about the experiences of West Indians, and that officials wanted to generate remembrances before time ran out. People who had trouble writing or were not literate might ask a friend or family member to write for them. Ruth Stuhl declared upon completion of the competition that "the Society is most grateful for all the entries and we regret that there could not be a prize for everyone."[2] Men of African descent from the British Caribbean wrote nearly all the testimonies. Their entries ranged in length and detail: some were mere fragments, a few sentences long, while others were six or more pages in length.

The writers in Box 25 constitute a small sample of the West Indian men and women who exerted a tremendous influence on the history of the Americas. Constructing the Panama Canal was a ten-year undertaking that generated several waves of migration and proved to the world that the United States was a dominant power in the Caribbean and Latin America. People migrated from dozens of countries around the world to build the canal, but the largest numbers came from British Caribbean islands like Jamaica and Barbados. The majority were men, many of whom signed labor contracts with the US government, while others traveled on their own to the isthmus to seek a job. Over time several thousand women joined them, working often as laundresses or domestic servants. Some brought children with them, and others gave birth in the Canal Zone, so gradually family life shaped the canal experience for many. These Afro-Caribbeans tended to be rural, leaving harsh lives working small pieces of land or laboring for large landowners. They boarded a ship for the isthmus in hopes of earning more money, acquiring new skills, or simply wanting to see the world. Many people think of these workers as providing the brutal, unskilled labor demanded by the canal project, and to be sure a great number worked as diggers and dynamiters. But over time Afro-Caribbean men often received training and began working at jobs originally limited to white North Americans, for example as carpenters or machinists.

Movement had long been important in Caribbean history, but this vast wave of migration to the Panama Canal Zone changed the Americas forever. Many migrants settled permanently in Panama, making that young republic a profoundly Caribbean- and African-descended nation. Tens of thousands more moved onward across Central and South America, the Caribbean, and often farther along to the United States after the canal construction was completed. The origins of the Caribbean American community in the United States are owed predominantly to the impact of these forefathers and mothers who traveled to Panama to work on the Canal. And as they moved, their culture and political perspectives—a hybrid of African diasporic influences and the impact of British colonialism—migrated along with them. For a relatively impoverished migrant group, they were unusually cosmopolitan and quite sophisticated politically, more likely to have received some education and to have navigated across different empires and work regimes.

To plumb the Box 25 writings for their full significance, this project traces the authors from their origins on islands across the Caribbean, to their journey to Panama and labor building the canal, onward to the moment of recording their memories in 1963, and beyond it to their struggles with aging and, finally, death. In excavating 112 individual lives and putting various archives in dialogue with one another, the book sheds light on the broader history of an often-anonymous group of laborers. The men and women who chose to submit testimonies to the competition were working people, often landless laborers or craftsmen. They traveled to the Canal Zone to escape harsh environments on islands across the Caribbean, where most earned wages so low as to be near starvation. They had heard about well-paying jobs helping build the Yankees' canal. Surely, they knew, it would be far more than they could earn in St. Lucia, Barbados, or Jamaica. They hoped they could save enough money to return home and buy a piece of land or open a shop. The men worked as carpenters, blacksmiths, railroad workers, gravediggers, salesmen, waiters, hospital attendants, janitors, and of course, diggers and dynamiters. The women most often worked as domestic servants in the homes of white officials or skilled workers from the United States. When the canal opened to great acclaim in 1914, Afro-Caribbean canal workers found other jobs. Some, including most of the Box 25 authors, kept working for the Isthmian Canal Commission, helping maintain the canal operations, while others moved home or onward to plantations across Central America, or saved their money and headed to New York City. Decade upon decade passed by, and in 1963 when the competition was announced, the original canal builders were now aged men and women. Those who submitted testimonies were most often male workers who had spent their lives in Panama or the Canal Zone. No longer working, typically confronting severe poverty as well as the ravages of time on their bodies and souls, dealing with disability and disease and sometimes the approach of death, they looked to this competition as a possible lifeline. They wrote up their memories or asked a son or daughter to write for them. They placed stamps on envelopes and sent in their testimonies with hopes the prize money would afford them a few days of comfort.

When Afro-Caribbeans disembarked from their ships and entered the Canal Zone in the early twentieth century, they confronted a sea of white faces. Their white bosses and supervisors were tough task masters. The United States developed the Canal Zone into one of the most modern and industrialized places on earth and sought to discipline Afro-Caribbeans into an efficient army of labor. US officials and foremen saw their Caribbean workers as childlike creatures who needed to be prodded constantly to work hard. The official government archives lump many thousands of workers together, melting away important cultural and geographical differences. Official government records, for example, typically labeled all these workers "West Indians" instead of noting that an Antiguan and a St. Lucian might not see eye to eye, or that Caribbean foremen and policemen, usually from Jamaica, were feared and held in contempt. Officials' lack of deep understanding of their workers makes their writings of limited use. The testimonies in Box 25, by taking us into life and work in the Canal Zone through the eyes and souls of Caribbean workers rather than their supervisors, provide an opportunity to recreate the experience from the perspective of laborers.

Like any archive, the testimonies in Box 25 emerged from a complex process in which personal experiences became entangled with the power dynamics of the larger world—in this case the colonialism of the United States and Britain, global capitalism, and the racial, gender, and class structures that resulted. How did those forces interact with the personal dilemmas of working-class Caribbeans and the vagaries of their memories to produce the testimonies? This book examines the processes and power relations from which the canal worker testimonies emerged and the subtle ways silences, inaccuracies, and neglected topics in diverse archives shape our understanding of Afro-Caribbean canal workers' experiences.

The canal builders left few accounts of their experiences, despite their numbers and their major role in building the canal. Most archival sources regarding Afro-Caribbean male and female workers flatten their experiences or erase altogether the complexity wrought by the diverse cultural and socioeconomic characteristics of their home islands. Government officials, medical personnel, white US housewives, and British globetrotters all published memoirs that bring the construction years to life. We can observe the project through the eyes of visitors like speaker of the house Joseph Cannon or presidents Roosevelt or Taft. We can pore over letters written home by a white US steam shovel engineer or other white working men. We can follow a census taker turned policeman as he crisscrossed the zone, sharing his opinions about details small and large, thanks to the book he wrote. But for those Afro-Caribbeans who so dominated the labor force, we have very little.[3] This makes Box 25 a rare source on the feelings and experiences of Caribbean workers in the Canal Zone.

Although typed copies of the essays in Box 25 are now available online, exploring the original documents at the Library of Congress makes clear the eloquence of many of the writers as well as providing opportunities for further analysis. Historians know there is something about that tactile experience—holding the letters the canal workers wrote and seeing the painstaking handwriting, some of which reflects their struggles with aging—that digital or typed copies can't match. Some writers included the flourish of a title page or a carefully penned heading that noted, "This is My True Story" or "Life on the Canal." Other essays were mere scribbles that are hard to read, perhaps with an apology at the end. Isaiah Bunting for example ended his missive by writing (in respect for the authors I will keep their original language, despite misspellings), "Escuse my Righten because I only have one eyes. I can berly see but prase god I am still living."[4] In some essays it is not difficult to sense the exhilaration their authors felt at the opportunity to describe their important contribution to the canal's construction. See the photograph below of the first page from George Martin's entry, which would win second prize in the competition: "On arriving at the Isthmus, had been like a new world, leaving my native land on August 27 1909." The online version of Box 25 also fails to capture one of the more unusual entries. Reginald Beckford found work during the construction era as a jeweler, and he not only described but illustrated some of his work. Some lucky workers would find a shark tooth after a dynamite explosion—from the days when there was no Isthmus of Panama separating the oceans. To show how he would mount the petrified tooth and make it into a watch fob, creating as he put it "a very good souveneer of the construction," Beckford included a drawing as illustrated below.[5]

At the same time, understanding canal workers requires placing their testimonies in dialogue with other archives. Since the authors were a small fraction of the total workforce, how did they compare to others? Were they more or less literate, younger or older, more or less skilled? Could we find the authors in other archives to learn more about their lives? In St. Louis, Missouri, the US government keeps personnel records it collected over the centuries on its employees, including the hundreds of thousands of Afro-Caribbean canal workers. I looked at thousands of records there, and with some digging I found many of the Box 25 authors—including Edgar Llewellyn Simmons, whom we met above. The US government had in most cases tracked and surveilled these workers for decades. Placing those personnel records in dialogue with the testimonies illuminated their lives and the stories they told. It also became possible, in many cases, to see photos of these

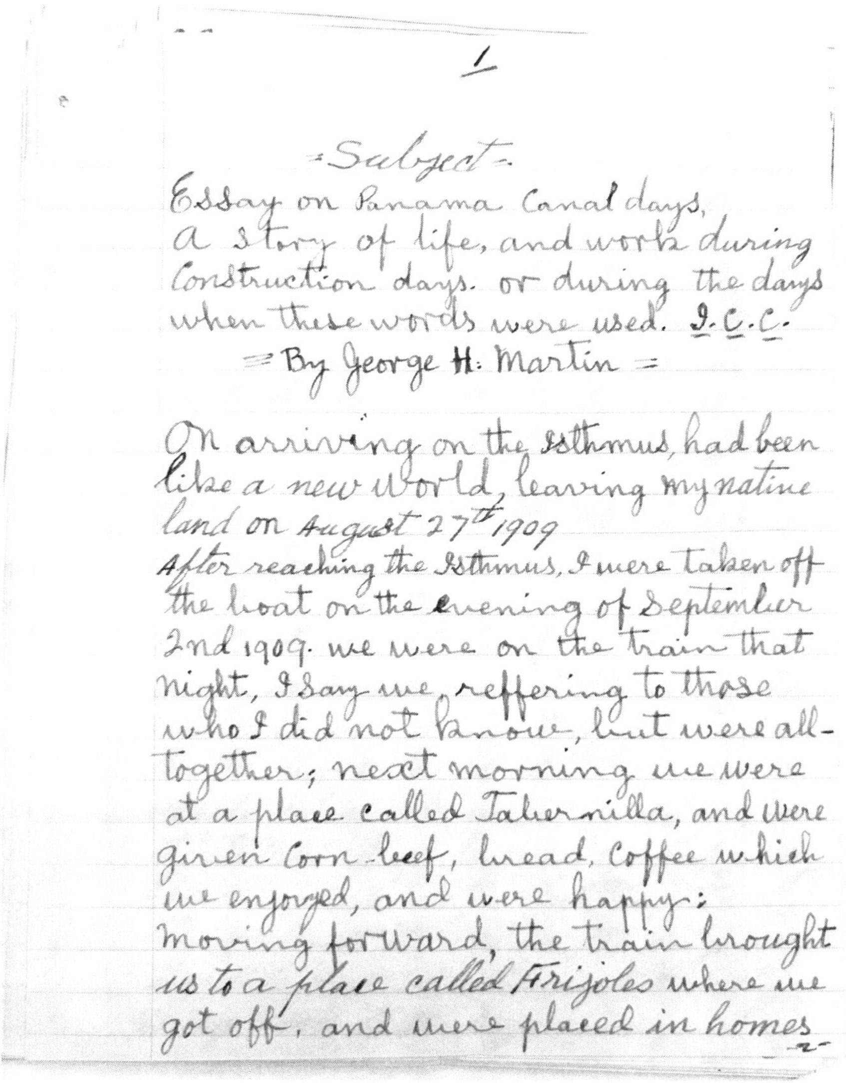

_1_

Subject -.
Essay on Panama Canal days,
A story of life, and work during
Construction days. or during the days
when these words were used. I.C.C.
= By George H. Martin =

On arriving on the Isthmus, had been
like a new World, leaving my native
land on August 27th 1909
After reaching the Isthmus, I were taken off
the boat on the evening of September
2nd 1909. we were on the train that
night, I say we, reffering to those
who I did not know, but were all-
together; next morning we were
at a place called Tabernilla, and were
given Corn-beef, bread, coffee which
we enjoyed, and were happy;
moving forward, the train brought
us to a place called Frijoles where we
got off, and were placed in homes

FIGURE 0.2 First page of George Martin's essay for the Isthmian Historical Society competition, Box 25, Canal Zone Library-Museum Panama Collection, Manuscript Division, Library of Congress

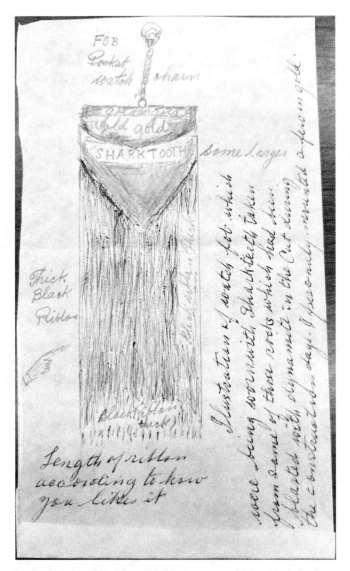

FIGURE 0.3 Reginald Beckford's drawing of a petrified shark tooth watch fob, from his essay for the Isthmian Historical Society competition, Box 25, Canal Zone Library-Museum Panama Collection, Manuscript Division, Library of Congress

workers whose words I had analyzed, bringing them more vividly to life. The personnel records thus created a wholly different lens for analyzing workers' lives, viewpoints, and the struggles they faced.

When we examine official government archives like the personnel records collected by the United States, we have to look through the haze of colonial condescension to reveal the lives of working men and women. Officials saw workers as a means of production to be managed, disciplined, surveilled, and then disposed of as easily as possible. Michel-Rolph Trouillot, Jennifer Morgan, Marisa Fuentes, and other scholars have explored the complex history of archival production, the ways archives emerge out of existing power relations, and the silences built into them.[6] They note the need to read archives carefully to comprehend fully the agency, subjectivity, and experiences of working people caught in the surveilling power of official archives. As Fuentes puts it, we must "account for the conditions in which they emerge from the archives."[7]

The Box 25 testimonies themselves tell a story of transimperial relationships, of Caribbean canal workers who moved through a terrain marked by the British and US empires but haunted as well by the legacy of the Spanish and French empires. The influence of the Spanish empire remained in the legal, political, and cultural structures of the Republic of Panama, while the tragic French effort to construct an ocean-level canal had transformed the landscape of the isthmus in ways that continued to shape the US project twenty years later. Afro-Caribbean workers carried with them a personal history of colonialism, manifested via the impact of disease and the remnants of scars from their labor, their bodies a "secret archive of harm," as one novelist phrased it.[8] By examining the historical production of archives related to Caribbean labor, this project calls into question the assumed stability of the official colonial archive. It asks how officials' misunderstanding of their workers as well as the demands of colonialism and global capitalism shaped the creation of the archives.

Yet the Box 25 testimonies provide a challenge somewhat different from the cases upon which so much scholarship about power relations and archives focuses because they were written by the Caribbean men and women themselves. These workers occupied a complex position. Their lives and aspirations were profoundly shaped by US and British colonialism and by their structural position within global capitalism. The competition was designed to frame, sanitize, and publicize the benefits of US colonialism. But it also provided an opportunity for Afro-Caribbean workers to express themselves, to create an archive that more faithfully reflected their own agency and

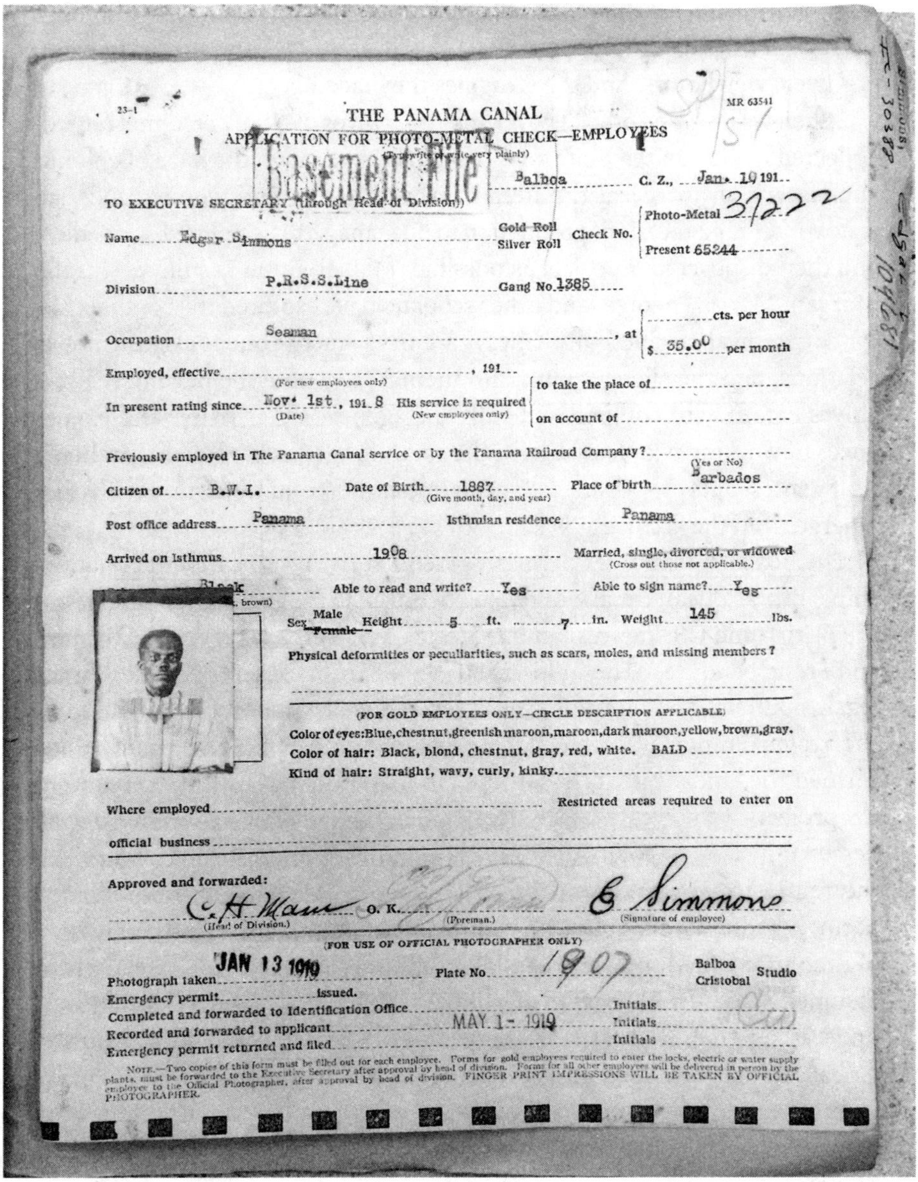
23–1 MR 63541

THE PANAMA CANAL

APPLICATION FOR PHOTO-METAL CHECK—EMPLOYEES

(Typewrite or write very plainly)

Basement File

Balboa C. Z., Jan. 19 191

TO EXECUTIVE SECRETARY (through Head of Division)

Photo-Metal 37222

Name Edgar Simmons Gold Roll / Silver Roll Check No. Present 65244

Division P.R.S.S.Line Gang No. 1385

Occupation Seaman, at ..... cts. per hour $ 35.00 per month

Employed, effective ....., 191.. (For new employees only)

In present rating since Nov. 1st, 1918 (Date) His service is required (New employees only) to take the place of ..... on account of .....

Previously employed in The Panama Canal service or by the Panama Railroad Company? ..... (Yes or No)

Citizen of B.W.I. Date of Birth 1887 (Give month, day, and year) Place of birth Barbados

Post office address Panama Isthmian residence Panama

Arrived on Isthmus 1908 Married, single, divorced, or widowed (Cross out those not applicable.)

..... Black ..... brown) Able to read and write? Yes Able to sign name? Yes

Sex Male ~~Female~~ Height 5 ft. 7 in. Weight 145 lbs.

Physical deformities or peculiarities, such as scars, moles, and missing members?

(FOR GOLD EMPLOYEES ONLY—CIRCLE DESCRIPTION APPLICABLE)

Color of eyes: Blue, chestnut, greenish maroon, maroon, dark maroon, yellow, brown, gray.

Color of hair: Black, blond, chestnut, gray, red, white. BALD

Kind of hair: Straight, wavy, curly, kinky.

Where employed ..... Restricted areas required to enter on official business .....

Approved and forwarded:

C. H. Mann (Head of Division.) O. K. ..... (Foreman.) E Simmons (Signature of employee)

(FOR USE OF OFFICIAL PHOTOGRAPHER ONLY)

Photograph taken JAN 13 1919 Plate No. 1907 Balboa / Cristobal Studio

Emergency permit ..... issued.

Completed and forwarded to Identification Office ..... Initials

Recorded and forwarded to applicant MAY 1 - 1919 Initials

Emergency permit returned and filed ..... Initials

NOTE.—Two copies of this form must be filled out for each employee. Forms for gold employees required to enter the locks, electric or water supply plants, must be forwarded to the Executive Secretary after approval by head of division. Forms for all other employees will be delivered in person by the employee to the Official Photographer, after approval by head of division. FINGER PRINT IMPRESSIONS WILL BE TAKEN BY OFFICIAL PHOTOGRAPHER.

FIGURE 0.4 Edgar Simmons's application for photo-metal check, National Personnel Records Center

subjectivity and made it possible to subvert the hegemonic narrative of racial capitalism and colonialism. The voices of the mostly male workers who entered the competition sing out clearly, articulating the deprivation and struggles they experienced. Analyzing the testimonies requires keeping this multiplicity in mind. The work of oral historians like Alessandro Portelli and Daniel James is helpful here, reminding us to be alert not only to the silences Michel-Rolph Trouillot analyzed but to inaccuracies as well. In the writing of both Portelli and James, it is precisely the moments when their subjects *misremember* the past that illuminate how power dynamics have shaped their historical memories. Just as silences exert causal agency, wreaking violence upon our understanding of the past, collective or individual misremembering and inaccuracies do so as well. Those moments provide a window into the ways individuals' structural positions in the world have contributed to generating their memories and understandings of reality.[9]

In all these ways the Box 25 testimonies illuminate the complexities of archival production and the ways they shape memories and narratives of the past. What gets remembered or forgotten, what gets deemed important or not, and how specific memories reflect not only what "truly" happened but also the narratives we construct about our own lives over time and the needs we have at the time of writing, are all important issues to consider. One might also ask, Is there something particular to the Afro-Caribbean diaspora, or to the conditions created by US power in the Americas at that specific historical moment that shaped which memories would be recorded? Other projects to record the stories of Afro-Caribbeans provide an opportunity to explore such questions. The Jamaican Memories Collection held at the Jamaica Archives and Records Department national archives in Spanish Town, Jamaica, holds entries to a competition launched by the *Daily Gleaner*, the major Jamaican newspaper, in 1959. Like the competition held by the Isthmian Historical Society, this one collected several dozen entries submitted as men and women recalled the Jamaica they had known in their childhood and early adulthood. Oral histories collected in Jamaica by Erna Brodber also provide a way to explore issues of memory. She conducted interviews with ninety people between 1973 and 1975 as part of her PhD dissertation in history completed at the University of the West Indies in 1985. Her interviewees included people in their seventies from across rural and urban Jamaica; transcripts of the interviews are now available to researchers at the Sir Arthur Lewis Institute of Social and Economic Research, University of the West Indies. The geographer Bonham Richardson likewise conducted interviews with Barbadians in the 1980s to help him write his book *Panama*

Money in Barbados and kindly shared his interview notes with me. Box 25 has benefitted from these different collections of memories generated by Caribbeans to contextualize what testimony the authors chose to remember, what they forgot, and what they got wrong.[10]

We can see an example of the limitations and inaccuracies in the Box 25 testimonies when considering the role of women. The testimonies tell us a great deal about male workers' experiences, but they are largely silent about women. Of the 112 people who submitted entries to the competition, only two were women. And those two testimonies are brief fragments that tell us very little. Mrs. Mary Couloote, for example, climbed aboard a ship in Castries, St. Lucia, with her sister in 1903. The ship took her to Jamaica and then onward to Pedro Miguel, where Couloote joined her mother and brother. Her brother was working at the Culebra Cut. Couloote visited the Miraflores asylum in search of a job, but the doctor asked if she had an elder sister. "He said to bring her for am to young has to handle those crazey women." When she got a bit older she found a job doing laundry for two American bachelors and then later worked as a domestic servant for an American family. After some years she got married and made money by sewing at home. Her testimony ends abruptly: "Then it happen a white man came and give every body notice that we have to live for the water is coming throw the canal and I move to Panama the year of 1914."

That is all we know about Mary Couloote. The other entry by a woman is even less helpful. It is signed by Albertha Headley, but she seems merely to have served as recorder for her husband, as it related his occupational history in a few sentences and some of the sights he saw while working. The men's testimonies usually mention women only to note their absence — "we had no women to do laundry," the men might say; or they comment that the officials "brought women from Martinique for us." Yet we know that women's contributions in the Canal Zone—and in the lives of male canal builders—were vastly more complex and important than those brief references would suggest. Understanding how gender, women's experiences, and family life more generally shaped life and work in the Canal Zone requires different archives than Box 25. Interviews conducted by scholars studying social experiences in Jamaica and the impact of the canal project on Barbados, by Erna Brodber and Bonham Richardson respectively, can be used along with US government personnel records to bring women's experiences to life. Joan Flores-Villalobos's recent book *The Silver Women* also adds immeasurably to our understanding of Caribbean women's important contributions.[11]

Another critical tension in the testimonies involves the Republic of Panama itself. The writers in Box 25 address themselves to the United States and say almost nothing about Panama. This reflects the complexity of the diaspora of men and women who worked on the Panama Canal, and the role of race in shaping power relations across the Isthmus of Panama. The colonialism of the United States and Spain, as well as interference by governments like France and Britain, influenced the young Republic of Panama. Both the Canal Zone and Panama manifested xenophobia and racism toward people of African descent from the Caribbean. Consequently, there are fractures within the category of "Panamanian" that shape how the history of the canal is seen, even today. The diaspora of those who worked on the canal stretches across Central America, the Caribbean, and much of the United States. The impact of the canal and the memories associated with it likewise cover a capacious geography and a world of lifetime experiences.

Perhaps one story will illustrate this complexity. In 2009, when my book *The Canal Builders* was published, I was invited by the US Embassy in Panama and the Museo del Canal Interoceánico de Panamá to give talks on the history of the canal. In Panama City I spoke at the Museo, a beautiful mansion that had served as headquarters for the French canal construction project. The large audience included an international elite of Panamanian society, including politicians and diplomats as well as academics and interested members of the public. My lecture focused on the ways that the important role of the Republic of Panama had been erased from the story of the canal's construction as a result of the legacies of US colonialism. The audience warmly welcomed me, and it was a thrilling night. The next day I traveled across the isthmus to Colón, an economically depressed city dominated demographically by Afro-Caribbean Panamanians, many of whom descended from the original canal builders. The talk was held in a public recreation hall that had seen better days, and the audience greeted me with some skepticism. As I began speaking about the important role of the Republic of Panama in the construction of the canal, people began to stir, and I could see a range of disinterest and dissatisfaction on their faces. They identified first and foremost not as Panamanians concerned about the legacies of US colonialism but as descendants of canal builders whose labor had not received sufficient recognition—neither by the United States, nor by Panama. I quickly shifted gears, put aside my lecture notes, and instead extemporized a talk on the "silver men and women" who built the canal. Immediately audience members' faces registered that this was the history they wanted to explore. They were eager for information about Afro-Caribbean canal workers. At the end they applauded my talk, and I had received a vivid lesson in the fractures of Panamanian society. This awareness shapes the pages that follow. As we'll see, those who wrote testimonies were predominantly Afro-Caribbean Panamanians, still ambivalent about the country in which they lived. The legacies of the canal are complex, and the experiences of Afro-Caribbean Panamanians are not necessarily the same as those in other regions of the diaspora.

I began this book project with a straightforward goal—to use the testimonies in Box 25 to bring to vivid life the history of workers whose experiences had been flattened or erased altogether from the official archives. I wanted to let the workers speak for themselves.[12] I wondered what we could glean about the worlds through which they moved by considering the testimonies in Box 25. Were these men and women typical of the Afro-Caribbeans who traveled to the Canal Zone? Could exploring their origins, how they lived and worked in the zone, and what happened to them upon the completion of the canal provide insight into the mobility of Afro-Caribbean working men and women? And could I learn more about these workers by tracking them down in the government's personnel records, which had never been examined by historians? I wanted to understand how they saw the radical new world they had entered, how they maneuvered to improve their working conditions, and how they connected to their own families, either in the zone or back home on their islands of origin. Over time these questions remained, but the project became a deeper entanglement with the mysteries of the archives related to the history of the Panama Canal. The narratives in Box 25 provide an opportunity to tell a story about the history of race and colonialism in Panama and the Canal Zone from the early twentieth century to the 1960s and beyond, to bring individual labor migrants' experiences to life, exploring their memories and misremembering, to consider not only silences but also the loquacity of diverse voices, and to place all of this in the context of power dynamics and the creation of archives.

By following the 112 writers of Box 25 from their islands of origin to the end of their lives, this book illuminates the migratory world of Panama and the Canal Zone with a focus on workers' strategies of resistance and accommodation. Taking seriously the power relations from which Box 25 emerged, we begin by tracing the creation and maintenance of US hegemony on the Isthmus of Panama across the twentieth century, as well as the struggles of Afro-Caribbeans against racism and xenophobia, and the complex views of Panamanians on issues of race, labor, and foreignness. Ironically, the Box 25 archive emerged from the white supremacist world of the US Canal

Zone, when a female librarian became sensitive to the struggles of West Indians and sought to capture their memories. Chapter two examines the struggles workers faced on their home islands across the Caribbean, the dynamics that pushed them to leave and travel to Panama, and the ideas and strategies they carried with them, the book underscores the diversity of labor migrants' experiences. In chapters three and four, as Box 25 authors encounter the Isthmus of Panama, we analyze how they compared to the broader workforce in terms of country and island of origin, level of skill, occupational mobility, the challenges they faced on the job—from disease to torrential rain showers and racist supervisors—and their strategies for negotiating with the US and Panamanian governments. In chapter five the book shifts to the US government's personnel records to examine how a very different archive expands our understanding of the testimony writers. The personnel records followed the authors over the many decades, to their final days confronting old age and impoverishment. A final chapter assesses the long legacy of the archive created by the canal workers. What difference did the testimonies make in the ways both scholars and the public have remembered and understood the labors that built the Panama Canal? To what extent have they kept alive the struggles of ordinary workers in building the Panama Canal? The challenge to sustain the memories and culture of West Indians in Panama is today more pressing than ever, but thanks to creative collaborations between librarians and the community of canal worker descendants, new projects have emerged to collect those stories. By following the writers of Box 25 across varied archives, from their early days to their final passing, this collective biography of Afro-Caribbean canal workers challenges customary understandings of labor on the canal project in numerous ways.

But first, by way of introduction, let us explore the testimonies of two writers in Box 25 who, together, raise key issues we'll encounter. While this book considers the experiences of all of the testimony writers, the life of one man—Constantine Parkinson—was particularly emblematic of the larger group. This is despite the fact that, unlike most other writers, he did not emigrate from an island of the Caribbean. Parkinson was born on November 12, 1894, at Playa de Flor, a Panamanian village on the far side of Limon Bay across from the city of Colón. In testimony submitted to the competition, Parkinson noted that "this little town was inhabited around French Canal days with mostly Jamaicans and few native panamanians, around the area was plenty of coconuts and some other fruits trees such as mangoes and pears." Parkinson's brief description suggests that the settlement owed its origins in part to the settlement of Jamaicans who came to work on the French canal. Parkinson's father, he tells us, was born in Jamaica, so we can assume that his father migrated to the Isthmus of Panama to work on the French canal project in the 1880s.

When the US construction project began in 1904, officials needed as many workers as they could get—even if it meant relying on children and teenagers. Constantine Parkinson began working for the United States at the age of 15, initially as flag boy with a survey gang. Parkinson found the job harrowing. For one thing, there were natural dangers. One day he ran down a steep hill, trying to keep up with the survey gang, and his feet got caught in a coiled snake. He called for help and men came with machetes to free him. Another time, working as rear flagman on a survey crew, he was standing all alone, knee-deep in water, and heard movement behind him. He turned to see a mountain cow heading straight for him. "I took my flag pole and run to engineer Mr. Bertartan and told him a cow was coming to eat me up." The engineer and some of the machete men investigated and found the cow had headed off and jumped into the river. Seeing how frightened Parkinson was, the engineer shifted him to a different job.

Like many workers, Parkinson changed jobs often, in search of better conditions and pay or a kinder foreman. He found work as a water boy, then back to a different survey gang, then onward to a railroad job. Snakes and mountain cows were likely the least of Parkinson's worries. Accidents caused by premature dynamite explosions, avalanches, or trains devastated the lives of many workers. One big avalanche near Gatun, Parkinson recalled, swallowed a group of Greek and Spanish workers; it took that day and night to dig the dead bodies out. Many of the dead had money tied around their waists for safekeeping as finding a bank was next to impossible. "It was a very awfull sight . . . but for many of us it did not mean nothing in construction people get kill and injure almost every day and all the boses want is to get the canal build." Likewise Alfonso Suazo noted the horrific aftermath of a premature dynamite explosion. "Como cogian esos hombres tomaron esos pedazos de carne humana y los depositaban en unas cajas y llevarlos al hospital de Ancon! No se si fueron quemaron o los enterraron." (How these men took the pieces of human flesh and deposited them in boxes at the Ancon hospital! I don't know if they were burned or buried.)[13]

Parkinson also recalled the challenge of working amid Panama's torrential rains and the threat of malaria. Like others, he complained about having to drink quinine every day and, during the rainy season, wearing wet clothes for days on end without changing because there was no sunshine to dry them out. Overall, he felt lucky with the bosses he had. Most people he met, he said, were friendly. Regarding leisure activities, he said only that every July Fourth the officials let them ride the train for free. "That day many of the workers get kill from drunkness cause hoping off and getting on while train moving."

Parkinson ended his two-page testimony with the story of an injury that changed his life. On July 16, 1913, he would have been nineteen years old. He had gotten a job as a railroad brakeman and was working that day at Toro Point, very near where he had been born. He provides few details but says that a train accident caused him to lose his right leg and left heel. There was no clinic nearby and no launch operator, so they transported him across Limon Bay to Colón, where a horse-pulled ambulance took him to the hospital. The doctors operated on him, and then here is the image that has stayed with me all these years, since I first discovered Parkinson's story: "After coming out of the operation in the ward I notice all kinds of cripples around my bed with out arms foot one eye telling me to cheer up not to fret we all good soldiers."

Constantine Parkinson remained in the hospital for months. When he returned home to his family in Playa de Flor he learned to get around on crutches. Months later he returned to the hospital to be fitted with an artificial leg. "It was a big day for me returning home as many said that I would not live."[14]

Like Parkinson, Jeremiah Waisome also grew up on the isthmus. He traveled with his mother from Nicaragua to Panama in 1895 at the age of seven months. Waisome remembered the chaotic nature of life and work in these years before the United States arrived. A man could work five different jobs at once and collect five paychecks, for the Panama Canal Company handled recordkeeping poorly. Due to constant social and political upheaval, everyone owned an American-made gun. Elections routinely brought violence. "My Mother would stock up supplies in her home in preparation for the elections, when the shooting start we had to lay flat under our bed pretty near a week, you could hear the bullits rolling off the roof tops."

Waisome began attending school, but at the age of twelve he could no longer bear seeing friends with their pockets full of coins on payday. He slipped away without his mother's knowledge one afternoon and approached a man in Balboa for a job as a water boy. The boss was chewing a big wad of tobacco, and he said, yes, I need a water boy. Like Constantine Parkinson, Waisome worked at a series of jobs over the next years, choosing some for their higher pay, but often finding a job dangerous and heading off to look for a safer one.

He worked as a switch tender on the railroad but found that too rough: "It means nothing to see men get kill daily, either by train, accident, or explosion by dynamite." One day he left Panama on a labor train headed toward Culebra Cut. Someone had accidentally left a dead-end track open, and the train, heading at full speed with ten cars of laborers attached, hit the dump cars parked at the end. Waisome recalled, "The engineer jump, the fireman got kill, and many workers got kill, one could hear the mourning and the hollering, that morning it was awfull to see the dead scattered around." Another time, men used tripod drills to load holes with dynamite. Around noon, as everyone was working, the dynamite exploded. Men and machines flew in different directions. "When the smoke cleared off, one could see human flesh dangling from trees nearby."

Jeremiah Waisome ended his account by commenting on his financial difficulties. Writing in 1963, he was now 69 years old. Like everyone else who entered the competition, Waisome had begun working on the canal decades before. These men as a rule were confronting declining health, many losing their eyesight or finding it difficult to walk. They lived in poverty and often used their competition entry to plead for more financial assistance from the US government. Waisome was unusual in still having a son in school. He worried how he would find the necessary money to see the schooling to completion. "Although it's a problem for me with my boy graduation coming up, but in God we trust."

In these two men's stories we see important aspects of life and work in the Canal Zone: accidents that crippled or killed, disease, poor sanitation (especially in the early years), rough working and living conditions, and pervasive racism. They had few resources to count upon for help. Like vulnerable workers across time and place, these workers relied on their own movement across jobs or residences to improve their circumstances. Friends and family also provided assistance. The silences are plentiful here as well. The men's writings tell us little about their activities off the job, their social and family lives, leisure experiences, raising of children, and feeling love or acrimony toward their partners. It's hard to tell from the testimonies how Grenadians or Bajans got along with each other, or with the St. Lucians, and is it true that most other islanders feared the Jamaicans? In the pages that follow we'll deploy other archives to explore both the substance of the testimonies and the issues the authors omitted.

But first, to understand how colonialism, race, civil rights struggles, and xenophobia shaped the writing of the testimonies, we need to examine power relations on the isthmus, from the coup that brought independence to the

Republic of Panama to the mid-twentieth century when the competition took place. The arrival of the United States as a hegemonic power in 1903 transformed the region and brought US and Panamanian history into collision with one another. Caribbean workers adjusted to a regimented landscape shaped by colonialism, nationalism, racism, and xenophobia. For its part, the United States remained eager throughout the twentieth century to present the canal project as an example of American ingenuity, civilization, charity, and technological and scientific advancement. At the same time, civil rights activism among Afro-Caribbean Panamanians in the mid-twentieth century not only generated new tensions but pushed a young librarian to imagine a project to capture the memories of the West Indian original canal builders. From these diverse currents emerged the testimonies of Box 25.

CHAPTER ONE

Colonial Power and the Building of Box 25

Between the US acquisition of the Canal Zone in 1903 and creation of the Isthmian Historical Society's competition for the "Best True Stories" in 1963, the character of US power on the isthmus, the challenges to that power, Afro-Panamanians' struggles to achieve their rights in the Canal Zone and in Panama, and US officials' view of their Caribbean workforce all changed. These power dynamics shaped the reasoning behind the creation of Box 25, the ways the testimonies were gathered, and the memories of their authors.

Most of the men and women who submitted testimonies in 1963 had lived their adult lives in Panama or the Canal Zone, working for decades for the US Isthmian Canal Commission. They confronted the colonial power of the United States but also racial discrimination and xenophobia in both the Canal Zone and the Republic of Panama. They belonged to Afro-Caribbean communities that fought for equality and acceptance and resisted the racism and colonialism surrounding them. By 1963, when they sat down to describe their memories for the competition, these workers had lived through decades of hard labor and poverty but also had witnessed a wave of global anticolonialism that transformed the relationship between Panama and the United States—as captured mostly famously in the 1964 riots in Panama City. The writings in Box 25, in short, reflected massive transformations of power as well as their authors' long lives of labor for the United States. To put the testimonies in historical context, then, we need to trace those transformations—from the building of US colonial power on the isthmus, to the Afro-Caribbean community's struggles in the decades after canal construction ended, and onward to the beginning of the dismantling of US power by the early 1960s. And in the middle of all this there appeared a young white American librarian who created the competition for the "Best True Stories." As her life and Afro-Caribbean Panamanian workers' lives intersected with these vast historical forces—colonialism, Pan-Africanism, and Panamanian nationalism—we witness the emergence of the archive of Box 25.

US power on the isthmus formally began on November 3, 1903, when Panamanian insurgents, backed by representatives of the New Panama Canal Company, rebelled to win independence from Colombia. US battleships entered Limon Bay to support them. On November 4, the United States recognized the new Republic of Panama. US officials immediately negotiated with representatives of Philippe Bunau-Varilla's New Panama Canal Company to draft the Hay-Bunau-Varilla Treaty. It established the Republic of Panama but also gave the United States complete and permanent control over the large stretch of land cutting across the heart of the new republic. That land became the Panama Canal Zone, in effect a colony of the United States. US sovereignty in the zone was complete. The treaty also gave to the United States massive power over the Republic of Panama, including the right to purchase or control any area within Panama if deemed necessary to the construction project, and the right to intervene militarily to restore public order in Panama. In the coming years, the United States dominated Panama politically, economically, and militarily.[1]

A few months later the United States began to flood Panama with surveyors, engineers, and mapmakers. Soon after them came soldiers, nurses, and sanitary officials to rid the isthmus of yellow fever and malaria. By the end of 1904, digging of the canal had resumed. Although the first years of the project saw slow progress and a rapid turnover of chief engineers as John Stevens replaced John Wallace in 1905, only to be replaced by George Washington Goethals in 1907, gradually the United States made its mark. Towns sprang up with housing, cafeterias, and hotels. Officials oversaw the building of police headquarters, fire departments, commissaries, and YMCA buildings, along with roads and bridges. Wider gauge railroads were built, crisscrossing Culebra Cut, where the Continental Divide ran through the isthmus. And as steam shovels roared across the landscape, as digging and dynamiting resumed at full force, the noise and the earth trembling amid dynamite blasts began to create a new sound, smell, and feel.

The construction of the Panama Canal required more than ten years' work by the United States and its global workforce, and it followed decades of failed efforts by the French government and then the New Panama Canal Company. It cost the United States $326 million to build the canal and involved as many as 44,000 workers at a time.[2] The United States not only dominated the Republic of Panama; its construction project transformed the nations of Central America by linking them more fully to the Caribbean demographically, politically, socially, and culturally. It profoundly changed many of the islands of the Caribbean, first by depleting them of a large number of laborers, then through money sent or carried home by canal workers and through a series of changes further generated by that money. The tens of thousands of migrants, traveling across diverse empires, nation-states, and regimes of labor discipline, gained a confidence and political worldliness that made them important players in the anticolonial movements across the Caribbean in the years after completion of the canal. Finally, the canal construction project also made possible secondary migrations, as many laborers traveled onward to Cuba or the United States after returning home to Barbados or Jamaica. In this way the canal construction project not only gave rise to a large Caribbean population in New York City, profoundly shaping the politics and culture of Harlem, but also linked the United States more closely to the Caribbean.

The United States created in the Panama Canal Zone an extremely hierarchical and authoritarian society that privileged white US citizens and carefully controlled the vast army of Afro-Caribbean laborers. Officials relied on a large police force, labor spies, banning of unions, and extensive powers of deportation. Most important of all was a system of racial and ethnic segregation known as the "silver and gold" dual payroll system, which paid white US citizen workers in gold and other workers in silver. It blossomed into a pervasive form of segregation shaping every aspect of life and labor in the zone. In some ways comparable to Jim Crow segregation in the United States, silver and gold segregation determined your job, what you did in your leisure time, where you shopped and lived, where you ate lunch, and—aspirationally, at least—with whom you had sex. The commissary, as we see in the illustration below, had separate entrances for silver and gold workers. For the several thousand gold workers, most of them white US citizens, life in the zone was in most ways superior to what they would experience in the United States, while silver workers, most of whom were West Indians, were paid far less, fed unappetizing food, and given substandard shacks in which to live. The racialized Canal Zone, a white utopia that denigrated its many Afro-Caribbean workers and residents, would generate massive struggles for civil rights across the Isthmus of Panama.[3]

From the beginning of construction in 1904, US officials focused on creating positive images and supportive public opinion for their project. US acquisition of an overseas empire stretching halfway around the world after 1898 had embroiled the nation in wide-ranging forms of intervention, from Puerto Rico and Cuba to Hawaii and the Philippines. The oppressive and, at times, violent domination this required called into question the benefits of US global power as a diverse group of anti-imperialists, journalists, and human rights activists began to criticize the military for brutal tactics. Formal colonialism in the Philippines became especially problematic from a public relations perspective. What began there as a war to liberate the country from despotic Spaniards became instead a military campaign to suppress the

FIGURE 1.1 The Isthmian Canal Commission's commissary in Balboa, National Archives

Filipinos' desire for independence. Soldiers in the Philippines wrote home to loved ones about their dismay as the enemy switched abruptly from arrogant Spaniards to the Filipino people, their former allies. As the war against the Filipinos stalled, the United States turned more brutal. Stories appeared in US newspapers of villages torched and water torture deployed against recalcitrant prisoners. This prompted congressional investigations and an energetic campaign to rebut the charges. Ultimately, it led President Theodore Roosevelt to declare premature victory in the war in hopes of silencing his critics.[4]

In this context, with its imperial ambitions under fire, the United States sought to ensure positive imagery regarding its growing global role. Among other tactics, this required differentiating the beneficence of the United States from the corruption of European empires. The French project to build a canal in the 1880s had failed spectacularly, nearly bringing down the government with it. The corruption led to trials and a five-year prison sentence for the engineer in charge, Ferdinand de Lesseps. Writing in *The Munsey*, a popular magazine, in 1900, one journalist noted: "The taint of a crime against humanity . . . clings about the memory of the Panama Canal. The word

Panama itself savors of a political intrigue, a financial orgy, and an engineering fiasco so complete as to be almost ludicrous." The plan of building an isthmian canal was impracticable, he noted, and ultimately dead.[5] Opinions like this one pervaded in the early twentieth century, so when the United States embarked on the project, many US citizens felt anxious that the Isthmus of Panama was a deadly swamp that would swallow their nation as it had France. There also existed significant skepticism in US popular and elite opinion about the project—concerns with the undemocratic way the United States had acquired the Canal Zone, for example. The United States needed to prove such worries unfounded and succeed at this project to broadcast to the world its rising global power, its technological, industrial, and scientific know-how, and its superiority when compared to the stale and corrupt European powers.

For all these reasons, officials cloaked the canal project in imagery linking it to the greatest triumphs of Western civilization. The famous poster for the 1915 world's fair, which depicted the United States in Panama as Hercules completing his thirteenth labor, provides a brilliant example of this. Officials also encouraged journalists to visit and write favorably about the project, and they sent government representatives and congressmen to visit and sing the project's virtues. Theodore Roosevelt himself played a major role, traveling to the zone in 1906 to examine the construction project and combat negative publicity about it. It was the first time in US history that a sitting president had left the United States. Roosevelt deployed his great charisma and media skills to promote the project, followed by an army of journalists. At every step a spectacle of canal boosterism and patriotism greeted Roosevelt. Canal employees greeted him with a "21-gun salute" of dynamite explosions when he arrived at Culebra Cut. He mounted a horse and galloped through the town of Cristobal, inspecting housing and cafeterias. Hundreds of mounted police escorted him as he entered Panama City. Throughout his visit, Roosevelt celebrated the canal as a spectacular achievement of American civilization and linked it to the virtues of the American republican tradition as well as patriotic duty. Answering one critic who had said he wouldn't want his son to work on the canal, Roosevelt retorted: he was "so impressed with the magnitude and greatness of this work" that "I wish that any one of my boys was old enough to take part in this work." He announced that US citizens who worked for two years or more on the canal project would receive a Roosevelt Medal in honor of their service.[6]

These strenuous efforts succeeded. The popular narrative regarding the canal became celebratory, anxieties about disease, corruption, or bureaucratic

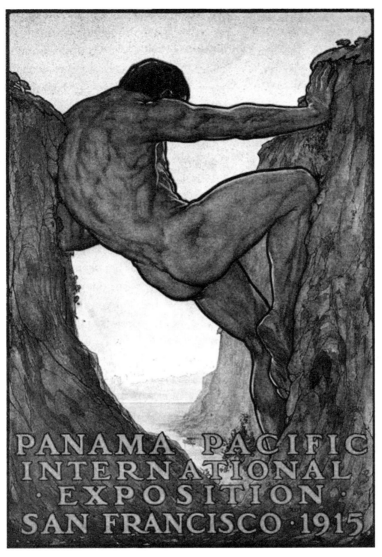

FIGURE 1.2 Perham Nahl's *The 13th Labor of Hercules* poster for the
Panama-Pacific International Exposition in 1915, The Picture Art
Collection / Alamy Stock Photo

inefficiency declined, and the Panama Canal became associated with all that made America great. As the *Chicago Tribune* pointed out in 1907, the average US citizen felt an "increasing enthusiasm and pride in American achievement" as a result of the canal.[7]

Articulating the Panama Canal as an exceptionally American project made possible by brilliant leaders required generating silences as well, which continue to shape the historical narrative around the canal to the present day. The first critical erasure involved the Republic of Panama. US colonialism involved not only the Canal Zone but also the nation of Panama. As we've seen, the United States dominated the country politically and economically. While Panama benefitted from the extensive sanitation work carried out by the United States (fumigation to eliminate mosquitos, building of sewers, etc.), it also became the site of much disorder and rioting as US employees and military personnel celebrated days off in the port cities of the republic. Often such disorder culminated in confrontations between the two nations, most notably in 1915. Riots that summer led to at least one death and resulted in the United States threatening Panama with invasion unless it disarmed its police.[8] Despite its essential role as host of the project and the myriad ways it supported the project (economically and politically, but also in housing much of the necessary labor force), Panama found itself erased from the dominant narrative. As the historian Marixa Lasso has revealed, US officials' notion of their construction project as modern required extinguishing anything perceived as premodern—including the history and geography of Panama itself.[9] When the 1915 world's fair, the Panama-Pacific Exposition, celebrated the triumphant opening of the canal, the US State Department refused to allow representatives of the Panamanian government to attend the opening-day festivities. Instead, a luncheon was held to honor the official representative of the Republic of Panama, Don Lefevre. He used the occasion to scold the United States for its humiliating treatment of his country. "I come from the country that made this Exposition a possibility," he declared. Lefevre implored his audience not to "forget the important share that Panama and its people have taken in this unparalleled undertaking. We have had our territory pierced in two through the powerful arm of Uncle Sam."[10]

The role of the tens of thousands of Afro-Caribbeans was similarly ignored by US officials promoting their achievements in Panama. Caribbean workers had been misunderstood and devalued by officials in charge of the construction from the beginning. John Stevens, the chief engineer who preceded George Washington Goethals, opposed relying on West Indians as a major source of labor. He pushed hard for the right to import Chinese laborers, believing they had worked well for him on railroad projects in the United States. When he finally lost the battle, he resigned. He considered Caribbeans to be "harmless and law-abiding" but also "childlike" and lacking in ambition. (He contradicted his own insulting description of Afro-Caribbean workers, however, by charging that they strategically and deliberately connived to do as little work as possible.) Similarly, attorney and Panama Canal lobbyist William Nelson Cromwell argued that the Afro-Caribbeans were "simple people" and "densely ignorant."[11]

Their desire to stress the technological, engineering, and medical innovations as central to the canal project led officials to downplay the efforts of all laborers involved in the canal. Numerous scholars have shown that Caribbean men and women were a force to be reckoned with in the zone, their actions and resistance routinely forcing officials to fine-tune their labor management policies in order to maintain a steady and reliable labor force. Nevertheless, the public narrative of the canal erased their contributions, presented them as passive if not invisible residents, and ignored the lively social, political, and religious communities they were building in the zone and in Panama. One can see this in the books and articles published during the early twentieth century that explored the construction project. *The New Story of Panama* (1912) by Frank A. Gause and Charles Carl Carr, for example, included only a handful of references to the vast army of Caribbean laborers, writing them off on one page as part of a "cosmopolitan community" where "American ideas prevail and American institutions obtain."[12] *The Panama Canal*, a popular treatment by Frederick Haskin published in 1913, devoted a brief chapter to "The Negro Workers" and itemized all their negative qualities: they were said to be physically weak, lacking in pluck, and unreliable. Despite this, Haskin concluded, the "Negro worker" proved himself to be a good workman although he was "shiftless always, inconstant frequently, and exasperating as a rule." On the other hand, Logan Marshall's 1913 book *The Story of the Panama Canal* managed to discuss the entire construction project with hardly a mention of the West Indians who dominated the labor force. Like the US government's official narrative, Marshall's stressed the technological, engineering, and medical achievements. Even a brief chapter on "The Labor Problem" focused simply on the challenges of feeding and quartering the tens of thousands of workers.[13] Such misunderstanding and erasure of Caribbean men and women's labor would shape historical narratives as well as official efforts to preserve a record of the project, with repercussions in the decades that followed construction.

These charged issues of representation framed understandings of US colonialism and its relationship to race on the Isthmus of Panama in the decades after construction ended as well. Racial discrimination determined
life for Afro-Caribbean Panamanians in different ways in the zone and in
Panama. The United States continued to segregate every aspect of workers'
lives and work in the zone via the silver and gold payroll system, while in
Panama itself Afro-Caribbeans faced hostility and lacked full citizenship
rights. By the 1940s and 1950s, however, a global campaign for civil rights
and anticolonialism destabilized the US colonial project on the isthmus.

Afro-Caribbeans were at the heart of increased tensions on the isthmus
in the mid-twentieth century. While the US government had encouraged
Caribbeans to return to their home islands upon completion of the canal, or
move onward to plantations across Central America, thousands remained on
the Isthmus of Panama. By the late 1920s, 40,000 Afro-Caribbeans lived in
the Canal Zone in segregated "silver towns." They would make up approximately 50 percent of the zone population in the decades to come. Everything
about their personal and work lives involved Jim Crow segregation: their work
environment, housing, and commissaries. At the same time the tens of thousands of Afro-Caribbeans living in the Republic of Panama (some 70,000 as
of 1920), many of whom migrated into the zone daily for work, also faced
intense discrimination and xenophobia from Panamanian citizens and officials. The Caribbean community in Panama grew larger in the 1920s and
1930s and built its own institutions and newspapers, engaging in what
Kaysha Corinealdi calls "diasporic world-making." They made Panama into a
central site of the broader Black Atlantic and made Caribbean culture integral to Panama. They expanded the social and political space available to
their community and fought for equal rights in the republic, particularly
through community organizing, a robust union movement, and the creation of news outlets like the *Panama Tribune*.[14]

Yet even as the Afro-Caribbeans in Panama formed a more rooted community and developed lively institutions, they confronted new efforts to exploit and marginalize them. A nationalist and xenophobic movement
emerged in Panama in the 1920s that portrayed English-language residents
from the Caribbean as undeserving and "un-Panamanian."[15] Acción Comu-
nal, an organization founded in 1923 by young professionals, called for
strengthening the Iberian culture of Panama and rejected the influence of
foreign people and their culture. In 1926 Law 13 was passed, which listed
Afro-Caribbeans as "prohibited immigrants" — singling them out for their
English culture and suggesting that Blackness was incompatible with the

Iberian traditions of Panama. In 1928 the assembly changed the Panamanian constitution to require that anyone with foreign parents must petition for citizenship after turning twenty-one. Another punitive law passed in 1932 banned several groups from immigrating, including Syrians, Chinese, and the "non-Spanish-speaking Negro." But the greatest insult came in 1941 with a revised constitution that denationalized anyone with parents born in the non-Spanish-speaking Caribbean.[16]

Thus, even as Afro-Caribbeans in Panama built a robust community spearheaded by middle-class professionals and working-class labor activists, they continued to face marginalization, heightened discrimination, and outright xenophobia and racism. They fought a two-pronged battle against discrimination and exploitation by the US government and its white citizens in the zone, and by Panamanian officials and citizens in the Republic of Panama. Afro-Caribbean Panamanians often felt invisible in terms of both the official public relations of the US-controlled Canal Zone and Panamanian media outlets. In the Canal Zone they struggled with assumptions that only white US citizens deserved consideration; within Panama they confronted suspicion due to their African descent and British-Caribbean background.

During the 1950s, however, as a wave of anticolonial and pan-African movements gathered strength around the world, so the dynamics of power within Panama began to change as well. The Afro-Caribbean Panamanian community became more skilled at protesting discrimination, but at the same time global anticolonialism generated a more powerful nationalist movement on the isthmus. Although these two currents of transformation were routinely at odds with one another (since Panamanian nationalism often manifested as xenophobia toward Afro-Caribbean Panamanians), together they began to highlight issues of equity and Panamanian sovereignty that in diverse ways transformed the position of Afro-Caribbeans within Panama.

This situation is analyzed insightfully by Kaysha Corinealdi in her book *Panama in Black*. The Remon-Eisenhower treaty of 1955 ended the silver and gold payroll system and stipulated that local workers would be paid at the same rate as US workers. The growing activism and prominence of Afro-Caribbean journalists, lawyers, community organizers, and labor activists helped make possible that landmark step toward equality. Corinealdi notes: "As the majority of the non-US workforce in the zone, [Afro-Caribbean Panamanians] formed a strategic labor group to court and a useful collective to exploit against Washington. Their struggles and discrimination under the zone labor regime helped unify the republic's treaty stance." At the same time, Panamanian officials and many citizens refused to deal with the everyday racism that Afro-Caribbeans confronted and instead demanded of them a "collective amnesia." "Even as government officials, including the president of the republic, called on Afro-Caribbean Panamanian zone workers to forget the past and work toward a new Panama, a looming question regarding citizenship rights remained unaddressed."[17]

Such calls rang hollow since Afro-Caribbean Panamanians still lacked full citizenship rights in the 1950s. Anyone with a foreign-born parent was required to petition for citizenship rights after turning twenty-one years of age. This rigorous process involved proving one's "spiritual and material incorporation" into the nation. Anxiety among many Panamanians about a potential West Indian takeover of Panamanian politics, a legacy from the 1920s, along with racialized notions that Afro-Caribbeans were loyal to the British government and could never be truly Panamanian, continued to forestall efforts to achieve full equality for all Panamanians.[18] In the face of continued discrimination, the Afro-Caribbean Panamanian community mobilized, using petitions, the media, and community meetings to fight for a constitutional amendment. George Westerman played a prominent part in the movement through his writing for the *Panama Tribune*. Finally in 1960 the National Assembly passed the Bazan Amendment granting full citizenship upon birth, and in 1961 President Roberto Chiari signed the law.[19]

The Afro-Caribbean Panamanian community's struggle for citizenship rights within Panama was interwoven with the fight for equality within the zone. In the latter, Caribbean labor activists were especially important. Eighty percent of the non-US citizens employed on the canal were first- or second-generation immigrants, mostly from the West Indies. Afro-Caribbean workers in the Canal Zone had attempted labor actions from the earliest days of the construction era, although initially the stark authoritarianism of the government and the surplus of laborers made it difficult to organize effectively. Completion of the canal and the outbreak of war in Europe maximized the strategic significance of the canal and increased the possibility of labor organizing. In 1916, 6,000 Afro-Caribbeans (approximately one-third of all silver workers) struck for five days to demand a wage increase. Authorities in Panama and the zone soon crushed this strike, but pay cuts, unemployment, and the spread of Garveyite ideas led to explosive protests again in 1919–20. A labor newspaper, the *Workman*, began to catalog the forms of racial injustice confronted by Caribbean workers. In this context the great Silver Strike of 1920 exploded, with 12,000 to 16,000 Caribbean silver workers demanding an eight-hour day, increased pay, equal pay for women, and a grievance procedure. This most powerful labor action on the isthmus during the early twentieth century lasted eight days and ended in disarray, with strikers fired or deported. Their union, based in Detroit (the Brotherhood of Maintenance of Way Employees) provided no financial support. Organizing for labor and racial rights remained an uphill battle.[20]

In the aftermath of this strike, in 1924, Caribbean workers formed the Panama Canal West Indian Employees Association as an alternative to traditional labor unionism. It would be the sole representative of Caribbean workers in the zone for the next twenty years, counting some 15,000 workers as members. Over the years it fought for improved wages, housing, schooling, disability relief, and sick and rest leave. It petitioned the American Federation of Labor twice for a charter in the late 1930s and early 1940s but was blocked by the predominantly white Metal Trades Council. In 1944 a new organization emerged that represented both Caribbean canal employees and teachers, the Canal Zone Workers Union. It petitioned the Congress of Industrial Organizations (CIO) for representation, and the latter responded by assigning the United Public Workers of America (UPWA), a progressive and integrated union, to represent non-US citizens in the zone, organizing them into Local 713. Canal Zone officials quickly recognized the new local union, in part out of worries that an even more radical union might begin organizing canal workers.[21] By 1947 Local 713 had 15,000 members and was busily organizing rallies and concerts for labor and racial rights. It demanded an end to the silver and gold payroll system as well as maternity leave, a single pay-classification schedule, a standard minimum wage, an improved sick leave policy, and retirement pensions. The UPWA also created, in the United States, a Citizens Committee to End Silver-Gold Jim Crow in Panama in order to mobilize for equality. The UPWA was a militant union. It refused to agree not to strike and focused heavily on racial equality, but such radicalism put it in a vulnerable position. Both in Panama and in the United States, charges grew that the union was linked to Communism. In February 1948 the *Panama Tribune*, led by George Westerman, began to sound an alarm about the Communist sympathies of UPWA leaders. This generated a bitter fight over labor politics on the isthmus, with local UPWA activists accusing Westerman and the *Tribune* of union-busting.[22] The *Tribune* continued its attacks, however, and pressure grew on the UPWA in the United States as well. In February 1950 the CIO expelled the UPWA, and CIO leaders then worked with Westermann and Edward Gaskin to create Local 900 of the Government and Civic Employees Organizing Committee as a vehicle for labor organizing in the zone. The fight over Communism badly damaged labor rights and racial equality on the isthmus. Edward Gaskin became president of the new local union and emerged along with George Westerman as a leading spokesman for labor and civil rights in the Canal Zone. Increasingly they also connected these goals to the fight for citizenship in the Republic of Panama.[23]

The struggles of the Afro-Caribbean Panamanian community against discrimination in both the Canal Zone and the Republic of Panama were intertwined in complicated ways with the growing nationalist movement in Panama. US colonialism on the isthmus was to some degree unstable from its very beginnings in 1903 and constantly in need of revision to sustain its power amid challenges from Panamanians and Afro-Caribbeans. The challenges grew more numerous and intense in the post–World War II era, as civil rights activism coincided with a global wave of anticolonialism. In the late 1940s President Truman ordered an investigation into segregation in the zone; the resulting report in 1947 by brigadier general Frank McSherry advised dismantling Jim Crow and the two-tier wage system in the Canal Zone—a recommendation that would be ignored for the time being. Paul Robeson visited the isthmus that same year to protest racial discrimination in the zone. The next year the United States retired the terms "silver" and "gold" and began referring instead to "American rate" versus "local rate" workers." And in 1956 the United States created a "Latin American School system," which involved adopting a Spanish curriculum for Afro-Caribbean students. Historian Michael Donoghue has found internal memos noting that officials saw the new system as a way to evade integrated schools in the wake of *Brown v. Board of Education*.[24]

The growing criticism of Jim Crow intersected with challenges to US hegemony across the isthmus. The Republic of Panama had bridled under US domination since the beginning of the construction era. Panamanians knew they benefitted in certain ways from the canal's construction, yet they also felt exploited and mistreated. In 1936 the United States gave up its right to seize additional land in Panama and increased its annuity payment to Panama. When President Gamal Abdel Nasser of Egypt nationalized the Suez Canal in 1956, he profoundly inspired Panamanians critical of US power on the isthmus. Protests against US hegemony began to increase. In 1958 Panamanian students organized a movement they termed Operation Sovereignty, planting dozens of small Panamanian flags throughout the zone. In 1959 an attempt by Panamanians (including the ex–foreign minister Aquilino Boyd) to enter the zone led to a riot, with protestors throwing rocks and bottles at US police. Ultimately tear gas and police dogs were used to push the protestors back into the Republic of Panama.[25]

Thus, well before the explosive uprising against US hegemony in 1964 that led the United States to consider transferring the canal to Panama, protest regarding both nationalism and racism were at a fever pitch on the isthmus. In 1963 the United States agreed it would fly the Panamanian flag beside the US flag within the zone. In preparation the United States began removing some of the hundreds of private and official US flags flying throughout the zone. When US officials removed the flag flying at Balboa High School, however, the white US students known as Zonians, long educated with a sense of their privileged colonial status, rebelled against the empty flagpole. They replaced the flag and then protected it, guarding through the night, to ensure no one would remove it again. Panamanians grew angry at this violation of the agreement, and when they tried to raise a Panamanian flag alongside the US one, fighting broke out. The spark to the explosive uprising had been lit. In the intense days of early January 1964, some 30,000 Panamanians, including many students but also a wide segment of the adult population, protested and engaged in violence. The United States deployed 14,000 soldiers and declared martial law. Panamanian protestors began setting fire to buildings, and snipers began firing at US military personnel. The US Army fired too, resulting in death for twenty-one Panamanians and four US soldiers. In the aftermath of the uprising, US popular support for Zonians declined. Lyndon B. Johnson in 1965 began negotiating with the Panamanian government to end US control over the canal. Although negotiations broke down, they would later bear fruit in the Carter-Torrijos treaty of 1977 that ended US occupation of the zone and transferred all control over the canal to the Republic of Panama. Today the Flag Riot is memorialized in Panama as an annual day of mourning—"Martyr's Day" on January 9—signifying the vast distance between the meaning and memory of the riots in the United States and in Panama.[26]

This torturous history of racial discrimination and colonialism in Panama and the Canal Zone, and protests against both, directly shaped the creation and maintenance of archives related to the canal construction's history. Yet the relationship between existing historical processes and the archives was complicated. An ambitious empire is a tremendous creator of archives, and so it was for the United States during the construction of the Panama Canal. The official photographer for the project, Ernest "Red" Hallen, captured approximately 15,000 images to document every aspect of life and work in the Canal Zone and beyond. The vast archives at the US National Archives in College Park, Maryland, document the history of the construction project in meticulous detail. Record Group 185 begins with documents related to the construction of the Panama Railroad in 1848 and concludes in 1979 when the passage of the Carter-Torrijos Treaty began the process of transferring control over the canal to Panama. The records break down every decision made by Isthmian Canal Commission officials but provide relatively few insights into the worldview and experiences of Afro-Caribbean male laborers. Information about Afro-Caribbean women is even more difficult to find. The US government conducted extensive surveillance of all employees and kept extensive personnel records, as we will explore in chapters to come. But in seeing the workers as objects to be controlled and disciplined, personnel records tell an incomplete story. The voices of Afro-Caribbeans appear more clearly in the records generated by the colonial and foreign offices of the British government because Afro-Caribbeans wrote to ask their diplomatic representatives for help and along the way provided much information about their problems and struggles. The documents submitted by the private detective assigned by chief engineer George Washington Goethals to investigate disputes or disagreements among the workforce provide a sense of the quotidian details of Afro-Caribbeans' lives, as do the civil and criminal legal records of the Panama Canal Zone.[27] Yet all these archives view Afro-Caribbeans through the lens of colonial hierarchies—they are records generated by social, economic, or political crisis or upheaval, of individuals caught in the gaze of the judicial authorities because they were alleged criminals or victims of crimes, or desperate men or women asking their consulate for help. Reading them requires analysis of the processes that brought individuals into the public record, which only happened when colonial relationships made them possible. Rarely could Afro-Caribbean men and women articulate their experiences on their own terms.

Government institutions generated all the above archival sources, so it's hardly surprising that they reflect the viewpoint of colonial officials. The Isthmian Historical Society, on the other hand, was created by white US citizens living in the Canal Zone—the so-called Zonians. During and after the canal construction era, life for Zonians became highly protected and, if accounts by the white Americans who resided there are to be believed, akin to a racialized, whites-only paradise. It was a sphere of complete government ownership; some called it a little socialist society. White Americans' world was insulated and isolated both from the racial politics of segregation that surrounded them (even as it shaped every aspect of their daily lives), as well as from the larger world of Panama. They could venture out and explore or shop in Panama but then retreat back to their cloistered experience in the zone. They made higher pay than they would have for comparable jobs in the United States, and when they needed something done at their residence, the US government provided the help. A good example of how many white US citizens perceived life as Zonians can be seen in the book by Herbert and Mary Knapp titled *Red, White, and Blue Paradise*. They called the zone the "world's first workers' paradise" and noted especially how egalitarian it was, almost without class hierarchy at all. (They noted that racial segregation was pervasive but bracketed that as unrelated to class hierarchy.) Zonians possessed a range of political beliefs, but generally the isolated, segregated, and relatively privileged lives they led resulted in conservative views that were resistant to change.[28]

Within the zone, libraries and archives played an important role in generating and preserving knowledge of the canal, its construction, and the social and cultural world of white Zonians. Libraries were also, inevitably, part of the boosterism associated with the US project to build the canal since its origin. George Washington Goethals created the Panama Canal Library in 1914. Over time it developed into a system of libraries—a main library, three branches, and five circulating libraries. In 1951 its name changed to the Panama Canal Zone Library-Museum. By the 1960s it held approximately 200,000 books, documents, maps, prints, and brochures. The Panama Collection within the library became one of the major resources for primary documents related to isthmian history, particularly the Panama Railroad and the French and American construction projects. Its holdings included personal papers going back to the mid-nineteenth century as well as materials related to social clubs and organizations in the zone. The key person in building this collection was Eleanor Burnham, who retired as library-curator of the Canal Zone Library in 1967 after thirty years of service. She was honored upon her retirement with a Distinguished Service Award and hailed for having "contributed immeasurably to the cultural progress in the Canal Zone," bringing "world-wide attention to the Canal Zone Library."[29]

The library's archival holdings reflect the colonialist environment in which they were generated, particularly the widespread determination to preserve the history of the isthmus but also to celebrate the US construction project and the distinctive quality of life and work in the Canal Zone. The library was theoretically open to anyone in the zone or in Panama, but in effect it was highly segregated like the rest of the zone. Non-US citizens were required to make a deposit in order to check out materials, while white US citizens had easy access to a library card.[30]

The Isthmian Historical Society, a social club founded in 1956 by prominent white residents of the zone, brought the testimonies of Box 25 into existence. The society's constitution noted its objective: to "promote and in-culcate interest in, and appreciation, study, and knowledge of the history of the Isthmus of Panama." It also sought to obtain and preserve artifacts and documents and sponsor public programs and excursions exploring the his-tory of the isthmus. In the following years the historical society became a cen-tral cultural resource for white Zonians. The society organized events that celebrated the history and legacy of the zone, honoring Theodore Roosevelt, for example, or bringing Maurice Thatcher (who headed the Department of Civil Administration for some years during the construction era) to give a public lecture. In 1958, to mark the centennial of Theodore Roosevelt's birth, celebrations were held across the zone to honor white US canal workers. Dozens of them returned to the isthmus for the event. As part of the cele-brations, Isthmian Historical Society president Loren Brodie Burnham inter-viewed thirty-five Roosevelt Medal Holders on tape, then transcribed the interviews and donated them to the Panama Canal Zone Library-Museum archives. The interviewees—male clerks, engineers, postmasters, and some of their wives—mostly recounted their employment history and a few vivid memories such as the exploding of Gamboa Dike that marked the completion of the canal. The interviews perhaps inspired a young librarian, Ruth Stuhl, to undertake a very different project a few years later: to collect memories of Afro-Caribbean canal workers.[31]

Ruth Stuhl's presidency of the Isthmian Historical Society, beginning in 1962, made the organization a more innovative force in Zonian society. Ruth Chevalier Stuhl grew up in the Canal Zone. Her father had left home in Ohio to join the canal workforce in 1911, working first as a policeman and later as a clerk. Ruth Stuhl's mother was a teacher from Long Island who, after teaching in Hawaii, met Ruth's father when traveling home via the canal. Ruth was born in 1929 in the zone, one of two children. Her brother, George Milford Chevalier, would play a prominent role in Zonian society much as did Ruth. Like many others, Ruth left the isthmus for the United States after graduating from Balboa High School. She attended both college and graduate school in the United States, earning degrees in library science. While in the United States she met her husband, Allen Stuhl, a minister; they divorced a few years later, and Ruth never remarried. She returned to the isthmus in the mid-1950s and became active in Zonian affairs. When elected president of the Isthmian Historical Society, Stuhl immediately began to formulate a more energetic set of goals and activities for the society.

From all reports Ruth was an independent woman. She traveled widely, undertaking backpacking trips in New Zealand on her own, for example.

Her niece recalls Christmas gifts from Aunt Ruth were never dolls or games but snorkels or sleeping bags. She loved the history of the isthmus and spent a lot of time "treasure hunting" with Panamanian friends, looking for artifacts or coins from early construction days. She wrote essays for the local newspaper recalling somewhat sentimentally life as a Zonian—the excursions folks would take, for example, or their ways of celebrating Christmas. She and her brother George Chevalier avidly hiked the isthmus, rambling along trails traveled centuries before by explorers and traders. They collected documents regarding explorations of the isthmus going back to the sixteenth century, recreated as many of the journeys as they could, and published a book about the various crossings. Ruth was an active member of the Panama Archaeological Society, serving for some time as its corresponding secretary.[32]

There are also hints that Ruth Stuhl was unusually progressive for a Zonian in terms of her political and racial views. One of her essays for the *Star and Herald* focused on the discrimination Afro-Caribbeans had faced in the Canal Zone. Although the essay included the patronizing attitude one might expect of a white Zonian, stressing as it did how much improvement had been made in the treatment of West Indians over the years, it also acknowledged that their wages should be higher. Most of the essay consisted of excerpts from a 1936 Labor Day speech by S. S. Whyte, the president of the Panama Canal West Indian Employees' Association, which described in detail the contributions made by Afro-Caribbeans as well as the exploitation they confronted in terms of low wages, segregation in education, lack of rest leave and pensions, and more generally the repressive policies affecting all West Indians.[33] Seeking further information about Ruth, I interviewed her niece, Michele Chevalier Hagerty, who grew up near her in the zone. She recalled that Ruth was supportive of the peace movement and the civil rights movement in the 1960s and 1970s. According to Hagerty, a rare conflict occurred between Ruth and her brother George when, in 1970, Ruth attended a rally with Rev. Ralph Abernathy, president of the Southern Christian Leadership Council, as the guest speaker. Ruth Stuhl took her niece with her, and Hagerty noted that her father was "not keen on going to rallies and such." But Ruth "was very supportive of Rev. Abernathy. She may even have brought him down to Panama, who knows."[34]

As president of the Isthmian Historical Society and, later, as librarian at the Canal Zone Library-Museum, Ruth Stuhl worked to document the history of the isthmus. She helped catalogue 16,000 glass negatives documenting the construction years, and she energetically pushed the US government

FIGURE 1.3 Ruth Stuhl, president of the Isthmian Historical Society, Ruth C. Stuhl and George M. Chevalier, *Isthmian Crossings* (Xlibris, 2001), back cover

to preserve sites of historical significance across the zone or repair gravestones that were falling apart. Looking over the records of the Isthmian Historical Society, one observes a significant uptick in its activities when Ruth Stuhl ascended to the presidency.[35]

In 1964, as the golden anniversary of the completion of the Panama Canal approached, Zonians mobilized to celebrate the date. By now, there were many challenges to US hegemony on the isthmus, protests had become common, and anticolonialism around the world increased tensions palpably in daily life. Afro-Caribbean Panamanians' agitation for equality had also intensified. The resulting tensions over Panamanian sovereignty made 1964 an opportune moment to highlight the grandeur of the Panama Canal's construction and yet also made for a more muted celebration as compared to the twenty-fifth anniversary or even the centenary of Theodore Roosevelt's birth held just a few years prior. Governor Robert Fleming announced, "At this milestone of service to world shipping, it is appropriate to look for a moment to the past . . . when the Panama Canal was a challenge, when its reality lay only in plans and hard work, thousands of men from many nations came forward to carry out the decade of labor that created this enduring work of engineering."[36]

Luncheons were held to honor the shippers who regularly used the canal as well as Panamanian officials and elites. A special award was made to the United Fruit Company as the top shipper on the canal over those five decades. Former canal officials and other dignitaries flew in to be feted. Officials organized a transit of the Panama Canal to allow visiting dignitaries to observe recent improvements made. They issued six new stamps to mark the occasion and created special medallions and booklets commemorating the golden anniversary for sending home to families in the United States. There were sentimental remembrances of the construction days, such as the *Panama Canal Review*'s essay on all the fun that used to happen on the Fourth of July—with no mention of the rioting and sometimes fatalities as canal personnel confronted policemen in the Republic of Panama.

Ruth Stuhl had a different approach to celebrating the fiftieth anniversary of the canal. Her viewpoint reflected the nostalgia and boosterism for the grand canal construction project that pervaded the isthmus, to be sure. Yet it also showed the impact exerted by decades of Afro-Caribbeans' mobilization for equality and the global battle for civil rights. Rather than focusing on the contributions of the chief engineer and his many officials, or the white US citizen foremen and engineers, Stuhl wanted to capture and preserve the experiences of ordinary Afro-Caribbean builders of the Panama Canal. "Very little has been written by them or about them," she said. Hence was born the competition that ended up in Box 25 at the Library of Congress. The competition would be open only to West Indians or other non-US-citizen workers during the construction era. In May 1963 Ruth Stuhl alerted editors of fifteen newspapers across the Caribbean about the competition. She sent ads to the *Daily Gleaner, Jamaica Times, Star,* and *Sunday Tribune* in Kingston, Jamaica; the *Barbados Advocate, Barbados Daily News, Barbados Observer* in Bridgetown, Barbados; the *Daily Clarion* and *Belize Billboard* in British Honduras; the *Evening News* in Port-of-Spain, Trinidad; the *Workers' Voice* and *Antigua Star* in St. Johns, Antigua; the *Vincentian* in Kingstown, St. Vincent; the *Voice of St. Lucia* in Castries, St. Lucia; and the *West Indian* in St. Georges, Grenada. In addition, society leaders put announcements about the competition in food packages sent to disability relief recipients in Panama and the zone. The ad instructed workers to give their name and address and place of origin when they arrived in the zone and what work they did. Stuhl set a deadline of November 1 for submissions and said she would announce the first-, second-, and third-place winners in December of 1963.[37]

Of the 112 entries, Ruth Stuhl chose sixteen contenders for best essay and forwarded copies to the three judges: Loren B. Burnham (previous president of the Isthmian Historical Society and chief of the Employee Utilization and Development Staff in the zone), Crede Calhoun (an ex-employee of the Canal Zone government and sometimes correspondent for the *New York Times*), and A. E. Osborne (an Afro-Caribbean Panamanian and assistant superintendent of "Latin American Schools" in the zone).[38] Many of the essays provided illuminating reflections on the construction era—in general they were far more informative than the tape-recorded sessions with "old-timers" from 1958. Judge Loren Burnham noted the themes he saw repeated most often in the testimonies: a pride of workmanship, pride at being part of the "great Canal enterprise," difficulty of supporting a family on low pay, and "satisfaction and a feeling of teamwork with 'good' bosses." We shall see for ourselves if this summary accurately captures the crucial themes of the testimonies.[39]

The society awarded first prize (fifty US dollars) to Albert Peters, originally from Nassau, Bahamas, but living in Cristobal; second prize (thirty dollars) to George H. Martin of Barbados, living in the Canal Zone; and third prize (twenty dollars) to Alfonso Suazo of Honduras, living in Panama at the time of writing. Each of these three individuals wrote stirring essays of several pages in length. Peters's entry eloquently told a harrowing tale of illness, interactions with doctors and nurses, and their successful efforts to treat him. Martin notably quoted from contemporary songs and included quite a bit of detail about everyday life. Suazo, one of the very few who wrote a testimony in Spanish, described the difficulties of life on the job. Clearly the job of judge involved subjective evaluations—there were many other essays as eloquent as these three. It's very possible that in awarding one of the prizes to a Latin American, the judges were acknowledging the continued importance of Spanish heritage in Panama. The prize money would have made a difference in the men's lives. Adjusted for inflation, fifty dollars awarded in 1964 would be worth nearly $500 today.

The testimonies remained in the zone as part of the Canal Zone Library-Museum until 1999, when the transfer of the Panama Canal to Panama was completed. At that point the entire holdings of the Canal Zone Library-Museum moved to the Library of Congress in Washington, DC. Today Panamanian scholars must travel to the United States to unearth their country's history, to visit the vast holdings at the US National Archives or the original copies of the Box 25 testimonies at the Library of Congress. To some Panamanians, the fact that the Box 25 testimonies reside in the US capital rather than in Panama vividly suggests the continued legacies of colonialism.[40]

In Ruth Stuhl we see someone shaped by her role in the US project of colonialism and the privileges allotted to white American citizens in the Canal Zone, yet influenced as well by anticolonialism and the global fight for civil rights for people of African descent. Such diverse dynamics shaped the lives of the generation of men and women as well who built the Panama Canal. The Afro-Caribbeans whose testimonies were gathered in Box 25, most of them born in the late 1880s and early 1890s, labored on the canal project and then, in most cases, remained living on the isthmus for the rest of their lives. They witnessed and perhaps participated in the rising labor activism in the zone and the fights against US hegemony and for equal citizenship rights for Afro-Caribbean Panamanians. By the time they wrote their memories down for the Isthmian Historical Society's competition in the early 1960s, however, they were confronting poverty and the infirmities of old age. All of this influenced what they chose to write. To fully assess the memories they shared, we need to go back to the beginning, to their lives on the islands of the Caribbean and their decision to travel to Panama to help the United States build its grand canal.

CHAPTER TWO

Homelands

Albert Peters, a young carpenter from the city of Nassau in the Bahamas, sat reading the paper one day: "I saw where they were digging a canal from ocean to ocean on the Isthmus of Panama and needed thousands of men." It was the summer of 1906. Peters was twenty-one years old. He talked over the news with two friends. "We were all eager for some adventure and experience." His parents opposed the idea, warning he would confront yellow fever and malaria, "but I told them I and my pals are just going to see for ourselves."[1]

Thus began Albert Peters's submission to the Isthmian Historical Society, which went on to win first prize in the competition. His words provide a rare glimpse into the thinking of a young man who made the journey to Panama. Most authors of testimonies in Box 25 say little or nothing about the islands from whence they came. In several cases we are not even able to determine individuals' islands of origin. We do know that the men and women who entered the competition came mostly from islands across the Caribbean. A few hailed from Latin American countries. Typically, like the canal workforce more generally, they arrived from Barbados or Jamaica. Others traveled from Antigua, Martinique, St. Vincent, Grenada, St. Lucia, Dominica, Trinidad, Honduras, Nicaragua, Colombia, and the Republic of Panama. What moved these men and women to embark on such an adventure? Although the dominant narrative typically conjures "West Indians" as an undifferentiated group, in fact there were very important differences in the factors on diverse islands that pushed laborers to travel to Panama. Likewise, migrants differed in terms of their occupations and socioeconomic backgrounds before leaving their island homes. Yet all of them struggled to make ends meet and were disenchanted with the racism practiced by the British Crown. The landscape of life and work on their home islands would profoundly shape their experiences on the Isthmus of Panama and generate important distinctions and tensions among the Afro-Caribbean workforce.

Although Peters mentions the allure of adventure, structural considerations also prompted labor mobility. Across the British Caribbean colonies, a small, white planter-merchant class controlled virtually all access to power, and Afro-Caribbeans worked long, hard days of agricultural labor.

With wages so low, starvation often proved a very real danger. Workers' connection to the British Empire came indirectly, via their labor within the dominant plantation economy. Most islands historically focused on sugar production, and most confronted economic crisis in the late nineteenth century as a result of competition from sugar beet producers in Europe and changing British tariff policies. Exports fell, causing even more economic distress for working men and women. As estates went bankrupt, several islands abandoned export-oriented sugar production, including Grenada (1890), Dominica and Tobago (1900), and Montserrat, St. Vincent, and Nevis (1920).[2] In Jamaica, some sugar estates went bankrupt, but for many, diversification became the key to economic survival: logwood and pimento production, coffee, and bananas. Banana production increased in particular, from 1 percent of exports to 52 percent between 1870 and 1910, while sugar exports declined in the same period from 45 percent to only 8 percent. Because sugar was much more labor intensive than bananas, the proportion of people engaged in agricultural labor fell significantly at the turn of the century (from 67.5 percent to 55.3 percent between 1881 and 1921), a trend to which the modernization of sugar production also contributed.[3] Comparing conditions in Jamaica and Barbados, the two main sources of migrant labor to Panama, reveals different responses to the crises of the late nineteenth century, as well as the ways these responses shaped migration patterns.

Jamaica's Morant Bay Rebellion of 1865 demonstrated ex-slaves' determination to fight for true equality in Jamaica, but the colonial government brutally crushed that uprising. In the decades that followed, a slowly increasing number of peasants came to own a bit of land and, typically, combined that with work on someone's estate to bring cash into their households. Afro-Jamaicans' landholdings were small and the quality of their land often inferior. Needing some cash for taxes and duties, farmers could not survive solely on subsistence agriculture. Some peasants, unable to own the land they worked, managed to squat on Crown land or lease a bit of acreage. A few achieved a degree of financial prosperity, enough that we might consider them part of the Black middle class, but the vast majority lived lives of insecurity. When they needed more cash than they could earn, they faced an exploitative credit system organized by shopkeepers. Planters were loath to let small farmers increase their acreage, and those who had to lease land faced the uncertainty of not knowing from one year to another whether their contracts would be continued. The sugar crisis of the late nineteenth century made life even more precarious: Work on estates became more sporadic, and the full-time agricultural laborers who purchased small farmers' produce lost purchasing power as their wages were slashed. Increased banana and logwood production, as the economy diversified, reduced small-scale farmers' access to land.[4]

Compared to other Caribbean islands, Jamaica had a robust Black middle class. In addition to relatively prosperous small farmers, professionals (teachers and constables, for example), and shopkeepers, there was a significant class of artisans: blacksmiths, carpenters, masons, bricklayers, painters, tailors, hatters, and shoemakers. Some of these trades declined along with the sugar industry, for example blacksmiths, but others expanded in the late nineteenth century. Overall Jamaica's Black middle class lost income in this period due to the broader economic crisis on the island as well as increased competition from cheap imported goods. Yet the vast majority of Black Jamaicans who worked as landless agricultural laborers fared worse since they possessed no financial cushion in times of need.[5] The urban trades became more attractive to those who could secure a foothold since the decline of sugar and the rise of banana production decreased the need for agricultural labor. Gradually urban populations expanded and with them the number of artisans, professionals, and small shopkeepers. The number of "higglers"— petty traders—also increased, providing a source of income for urban women in particular.[6]

In all these ways, conditions in Jamaica differed from those in Barbados, the other island that sent the most laborers to Panama. If anything, the plantation system in Barbados proved to be crueler than that of Jamaica. Black Barbadians were more completely entrapped in landless agricultural labor. The plantation elite in Barbados strenuously resisted selling even small pieces of land to laborers, preferring to maintain an agricultural proletariat with few options. There were no Crown lands upon which laborers might squat as in Jamaica. Indeed, according to historian Hilary Beckles, the government and planters collaborated in over appraising the value of land to keep it out of the hands of Black Barbadians. The typical Barbadian thus rented a small chattel house and a quarter acre of land for growing some food but relied primarily upon cash wages earned by laboring on a neighboring sugar estate. Only a precious few people escaped their fate as landless laborers. This not only constrained the amount of surplus income available to the Black population as a whole but also suppressed the development of a robust professional or artisanal class. Similar conditions characterized Antigua and St. Kitts, where, as in Barbados, sugar production dominated the economy into the twentieth century and employed most of the Black population.[7]

The sugar crisis hit Barbados as it did Jamaica, but with a different consequence. Estates that were put on the market were typically purchased by resident merchants (there was strong and effective resistance to absentee landlords in Barbados), leading to the creation of a new merchant-planter elite. And rather than diversify as in Jamaica, Barbadian planters instead further impoverished their laborers to make ends meet. Poverty had long been a favored form of discipline, with planters believing that laborers would become idle as soon as they had enough food to eat. But when economic crisis hit in the late nineteenth century, lasting well into the twentieth, planters who faced decreased profits responded by slashing wages. The 1897 Royal Commission investigating the sugar industry concluded that the laboring population was bearing the brunt of the crisis. Planters cut wages by 30 percent, pushing workers below starvation level. The commission encouraged policies that would make possible the rise of a peasant class, but as before, Barbadian planters and the government both opposed this. Mortality rates and malnutrition rose, and when disease hit (such as typhoid and dysentery after the 1898 hurricane, smallpox in 1902–03, and yellow fever in 1908) the laboring classes suffered mightily. Reports circulated of starvation across the countryside, and food scavenging became common. With the high population density on the island (highest in the West Indies) and no available land on which to take refuge, laborers had few options. Sporadic outbreaks of protest occurred. Workers engaged repeatedly in potato raids during the 1880s and 1890s, cane fires occurred daily, and broader riots and social unrest became endemic.[8]

If Barbados and Jamaica thus represented two divergent histories of economic transformation resulting from sugar crisis and its impact on Black workers, other islands supplying workers for the Panama Canal fell somewhere between the two. Most, like Jamaica, experienced a strengthening of the peasant class. But across the British Caribbean, as economic crisis hit and life became more challenging for Black workers, migration as a means of escape became more appealing. From the days of enslavement onward, internal migration and emigration had been key strategies for islanders locked into poverty and backbreaking labor, and colonial governments had encouraged this to varying degrees.[9] Upon (final) emancipation in 1838, some Barbadians had migrated from rural to urban areas of the island, particularly during times of economic trouble, and they emigrated to British Guiana and Trinidad as well to seek the higher wages offered there. Jamaicans likewise emigrated in small numbers throughout the nineteenth century, with 1,500 to 2,000 traveling to the Isthmus of Panama to help build the first transcontinental railroad in the 1850s. In the 1880s, Jamaicans provided the French with a major source of labor during their doomed effort to build a canal across Panama, and a smaller number of Jamaicans traveled to Costa Rica for railroad construction jobs. Although it is difficult to estimate precisely how many emigrated during the decade, colonial office records show that 84,163 people departed Jamaica during the 1880s. In 1888 when the French canal project failed, thousands of stranded Jamaicans on the isthmus relied upon the Jamaican government for repatriation, at great expense to the latter.[10] The massive emigration also caused acute labor shortages for Jamaican planters. Consequently, the Jamaican government passed laws to prevent further exoduses on this scale. The most important was Law 23, passed in 1902, which allowed the government to require that an exit permit be purchased for twenty-five shillings.[11]

When the United States in 1903 began planning its own canal construction project—and locating a source of labor loomed large—officials at first sought white Europeans or Chinese laborers, but both turned out to be unfeasible (white Europeans were too expensive, and anti-Chinese laws in both Panama and the United States disallowed the importation of Chinese laborers). Turning to Caribbeans as a source of labor, the United States immediately had to contend with the priorities of the British Empire, and officials found negotiating difficult with many of the colonial governments. Although US officials promised Jamaican officials that their men would be treated well—even offering to hire Jamaicans as foremen so they would not have to work under Americans—because of the crisis that had followed the collapse of the French canal effort, the latter refused to allow a recruiting station on the island and adhered to the law requiring twenty-five shillings for an exit permit. Other island governments, including St. Kitts, Antigua, Montserrat, and Grenada, likewise refused to allow recruiting agents in their domains. R. E. Wood, the recruiting agent for the US government, observed to his dismay that recruiters were forced to "wander from island to island, picking up men here and there, like discredited fugitives."[12]

These circumstances made Barbados an especially important source for labor. Its colonial government was agreeable to labor recruitment, and the island had a surplus of English-speaking laborers whom US recruiters considered polite, obedient, and orderly. As early as 1893 the Barbadian colonial government had begun to consider sponsored emigration schemes as a safety valve that could help their impoverished laborers. In 1894 the colonial secretary commented on an unusual rise in mortality among Afro-Caribbeans with a stark, Darwinian warning: "It means that nature is exerting herself in a very unmistakable way; that the fight for life is getting sharper and that when hard times come, and their shadow is at our doors, the difficulties will become accentuated. No doubt in theory the weak will disappear before the strong."[13] The government sought to help the weak survive merely by encouraging emigration.

After US officials presented a sample labor contract, Barbadian government officials allowed construction of a recruiting station on the island. The United States offered free transportation, a labor contract, and free passage home after 500 days of work. Ironically, in bringing tens of thousands of contract laborers to Panama the United States violated its own Alien Contract Law of 1885 (also known as the Foran Act), which prohibited bringing unskilled laborers to the United States on contracts. Nonetheless, the Barbados recruiting station, established in 1905, was within a year or two sending several ships a week to Panama. Laborers made a mass exodus from the estates, creating a remarkable sight as they marched across the island to Bridgetown. People began to speak of a fever for traveling to Panama. To many men who signed contracts for Panama, the attraction was certainly a desire to throw off the yoke of impoverishment, exploitation, and backbreaking work on plantations. Planters expressed dismay at the large number of laborers heading to the recruiting office. Police struggled to maintain order as thousands arrived at a time. One man heading with other laborers to Bridgetown shouted to a gang of sugar workers, "Why you don't hit de manager in de head, and come along wid we!"[14]

As word of the job opportunities spread across the Caribbean, workers traveled to Bridgetown from other islands in hopes of securing a contract and passage to Panama. Gradually Barbadians who could not win a contract, including women and children, began saving money to pay their own way to Panama. Such strategies make it difficult to determine with precision how many workers from Barbados ultimately traveled to work on the canal. Bonham Richardson estimated that 20,000 (male) contract laborers traveled from Barbados to Panama, and as many as 40,000 more men and women traveled without a labor contract: a remarkable number considering that Barbados's population at the time was only some 180,000. The Panama movement constituted the largest emigration in Barbadian history. Those who stayed in Barbados used the new labor scarcity to bargain for higher wages, and planters resisted this by hiring women to do work previously assigned to men. As Bonham Richardson has demonstrated, Barbadians in Panama sent home remittances (nearly 546,000 pounds) and returned home with money that allowed a significant number of people to purchase land and achieve

[Cooper Photo.

DEPARTURE OF LABOURERS FROM BARBADOS FOR THE PANAMA CANAL.

FIGURE 2.1 Departure of laborers from Barbados for the Panama Canal, 1909, New York Public Library Digital Collections

economic independence. In these ways, the Panama movement exerted a seismic impact on Barbadian society.[15]

Transimperial labor recruiting proved more difficult in the case of Jamaica. Secretary of war William Howard Taft tried unsuccessfully to negotiate with the government of Jamaica to recruit contract laborers there. The Jamaican government would not allow its citizens to become contract laborers for the canal unless the United States agreed to pay insurance for each individual. In a December 1904 meeting in Kingston, with British consul Claude Mallet and governor of Jamaica Alexander Swettenham in attendance, chief engineer John Wallace worried that paying an insurance fee would make the deal appear to be labor trafficking. Similarly, Governor Swettenham declared that any time insurance was paid, the deal might appear like trafficking. According to John Wallace, the stipulation that the US government provide funds for repatriation could also cause laborers to break their contract early at great cost to the United States. In response Swettenham made the draconian suggestion that the United States sentence those who failed to finish their contract to a term in the penitentiary. In the end the negotiations failed, the Jamaican government refused to allow a recruiting office on the island, and Jamaicans who sought to leave for the Canal Zone were required to pay the twenty-five-shilling tax for an emigration permit.[16]

Despite these obstacles, Jamaicans headed to Panama in large numbers, as many as 80,000 making their way there. The Jamaican author Herbert G. De Lisser alluded to challenges faced by the migrants who traveled alongside him to Panama in 1910: "For weeks and months before they left their homes they had been thinking of this voyage and preparing for it. They had saved a little money, but most likely had found it was not enough; so the household gods were sacrificed, the chairs and tables, perhaps even the bed, had to be sold before the necessary sum could be made up to pay for the passage and to lodge in the Treasury the 25s. demanded by the Government for repatriation purposes." The financial requirement ensured that those who departed Jamaica possessed more financial resources than did men and women from other islands. Consequently, the profile of the typical Jamaican who headed to Panama was distinctive: few were landless laborers; most were artisans, small shopkeepers, and peasants who owned some land. When Jamaicans arrived in Panama, as a result, they were more likely to acquire jobs as craftsmen, foremen, teachers, or policemen. Tracking the writers in Box 25, and examining hundreds of other individuals' records as well through the personnel records of the US government confirms this. The Jamaicans were most likely to hold skilled and lucrative occupations: artisans, boatmen, messengers, clerks, and railroad workers, for example. Reports from Jamaica also confirmed that those workers who returned home after construction ended often displayed their wealth conspicuously. Jamaicans recalled decades later how the men returning from Panama often flashed gold teeth or a gold watch and chain.[17]

Of the tens of thousands of men and women who traveled to the Canal Zone from the islands of the Caribbean, many traveled on their own while others made the trip to Bridgetown and signed a labor contract with the US government. However they journeyed, they sold belongings and packed bags for an uncomfortable journey across the sea to Panama. Harrigan Austin, among the first to depart for Panama, left Bridgetown in October 1905 for a "hazardous trip, of thirteen days of bad weather, bad accommodation in general with sparing meals on a Crowded Ship, we were all more or less hungry." Mary Couloote left her home in Castries, St. Lucia, traveling on the ship

La Plata along with a sister. They stopped in Jamaica and then headed across the Gulf of Mexico. When a heavy storm hit, crew members ordered everyone downstairs to second class where it would be safer. She remembered, "The sailor had chain around they waist and a pail emptying out the water when we reach colon they call everybody name 5 men where missing from Jamaica." Undoubtedly relieved to arrive, Couloote headed to Pedro Miguel to join her mother and brother.[18] Philip McDonald's journey demonstrates the roundabout route some took. At the age of eighteen he left his home in Grenada, on May 18, 1908, for Trinidad. There he met the *SS Magdalena* arriving from Bridgetown and filled with hundreds of Barbadians. "It was the first time in my life I ever saw such a crowd of Barbadians together." The ship steamed toward the isthmus, making two other stops before reaching Colón on June 1. The migrants received no food while in transit, and sleeping accommodations were also not provided (if possible, migrants brought deck chairs—called stretchers—on board for that purpose). The Englishwoman Winifred James traveled to Panama on board a ship with many West Indians and observed, "The West Indian negro has a passion for travelling. . . . You see the streams of them getting on and off at every port. Up the gangways they file solemnly, one behind the other, carrying their bundles and their stretchers. The traveling kit of the decker is well worth seeing. A canvas stretcher on folding legs, a magnificent white-frilled cushion, a number of bursting brown-paper parcels and a kerosene tin." The tins, she added, are referred to as the "negro's steamer trunk."[19]

The migrants climbing aboard ships to Panama were typically young men and women in their late teens and early twenties. They had grown up in a culture where emigration was an important life strategy; most knew relatives or family friends who had left their home islands for work across the Caribbean and Central America, if not farther afield. A sense of cosmopolitanism was in the air they breathed. And they undoubtedly found pleasure in fleeing the hard lives ahead of them, mired in colonial exploitation, racism, and impoverishment as landless laborers in Barbados or St. Lucia, or as peasants struggling to make ends meet in Jamaica.

John Altyman Richards explained the appeal of Panama in his competition entry: "Many years ago while still yet a young man in Jamaica I was intrigued by the Canal Construction done in this beautiful tropical country. I discussed the possibilities of working in a different country and of learning a strange language with my relatives; as soon as permission was granted I partook for Panama in 1914." Like other migrants across time and place, Richards had surveyed his current life and determined that Panama beckoned as an im-

84-D. Arrival at Cristobal of S.S. Ancon with 1500 Laborers from Barbado[.] Deck Scene, Sept. 2, 1909.

FIGURE 2.2 Ship with Barbadians arriving in Cristobal, Panama, 1909, National Archives

provement. He'd have access there to good Yankee jobs building the canal. Migrants could make enough money to open a business or buy some land upon their return. As Herbert De Lisser wrote, "The West Indian peasant dreams of Panama as the country where fortune awaits him, and where a few months of effort will bring a golden reward."[20] The same held true for those who traveled to Panama not for canal jobs but to create their own businesses. Thus E. W. Martineau, for example, left his home in Grenada equipped with aerated water equipment to set up shop as a soda factory. He modeled his decisions on his parents' approach to life: "My father before me was a man of very gentle character, very kind in his ways and action; he would even give up his rights for peace sake, he was too soft in his day to accumulate wealth, therefore he died poor. My Mother was just the opposite, she was loving and kind to her home circle, but she was very stern in business, and upright with individuals. She would go to any extent to obtain her right, if she thought she was right." Martineau saw his own identity, he explained, as a "peculiar combination" of the two parents, and this led him to the adventure of making a name for himself in Panama.[21]

Hopes for economic opportunity certainly pushed migrants like these to the Canal Zone as they sought to escape the extreme poverty on their home islands. In addition, Afro-Caribbeans had ample reason to feel let down by the British Crown. The racist and undemocratic structures of colonialism, the oppression exerted by the planter elite, and the devastation caused by economic crisis all suggested their denial of rights as British subjects. Furthermore, on these islands the enslavement of men and women was not too distant a memory. One Jamaican recalled his days as a young boy in the 1870s, when many ex-enslaved men were still alive. Every August 1, the town of Negril would gather at the Presbyterian chapel to sing hymns and hear a sermon about life under slavery. Then some of the freedmen would climb up on the stage to tell stories of their lives. Afterward everyone would adjourn outside for a feast, drinks, and dancing to celebrate emancipation.[22]

In this environment, with enslavement a close memory and landlessness offering little beyond toil and impoverishment, the planter elite strenuously promoted a cult of the British Empire and the monarchy as a glue that might hold society together. As Brian Moore and Michele Johnson have explained, the lower classes were "encouraged to remember they were part of a mighty whole, at the centre of which was a power so distant yet so omnipotent and worthy that only displays of adoration were deemed appropriate."[23] Planters celebrated love and loyalty to the mother country and the queen as central to notions of respectability and civilization. Although one should not exaggerate the degree to which imperial and monarchic fervor pervaded the lower classes of the islands, it is clear that Afro-Caribbeans shared in pride of British culture, education, and language. Furthermore, they had their own reasons for royalist Anglophilia: historians have observed that Afro-Caribbeans linked the emancipation of slaves to Queen Victoria. Great sadness pervaded the islands when Queen Victoria died in 1901. Upon her death Victoria Day was changed to Empire Day, and efforts to inculcate in children a pride in British imperialism and a strong connection to the mother country grew even more robust. As we will see, imperial allegiances could also provide a resource for British West Indians once they arrived in Panama.[24]

The ships steaming toward the Isthmus of Panama, then, brought young emigrants carrying wide-ranging ideas and loyalties in addition to their bags and deck chairs. Thousands began to arrive from Jamaica, Barbados, and smaller islands. Although as a general rule they all struggled under the weight of the white British planter-merchants who controlled their islands, they varied considerably in their economic fortunes and levels of skill. Jamaicans in particular arrived in Panama with more diverse backgrounds and more financial and occupational resources. But West Indians shared in common strategies they had developed for coping with the brutal racism of the British Empire. As they entered the Canal Zone with its harsh industrial discipline, Caribbeans' loyalty to king and empire would become entangled with new strategies they developed to resist exploitation at the hands of American officials.

CHAPTER THREE

Encountering Panama

Harrigan Austin boarded the Royal Mail steamship *Orinoco* in Bridgetown in October 1905. A stocky young man only eighteen years old, Austin had been born in Saint Andrews, a rural parish of rolling green hills in northeastern Barbados. His trip to Colón was difficult and slow, with bad weather and insufficient food. Upon arrival, he said, "We were more or less hungry." As they disembarked, the men saw bags of brown sugar on the dock. "And the whole crowd of us like ants fed ourselves on that sugar without questioning any one, and no one said anything to us either."[1] After the men ate their fill, they climbed aboard freight trains to travel to their cots in the open air. Accommodations remained highly rustic in those early days, particularly for Caribbean workers.

Austin came to Panama armed with carpenter's tools, so he was a lucky one assigned from the start to a trade. This meant his working conditions and wages would both be better than normal. Despite this, Austin found the work hard. The men worked through bad weather, including Panama's torrential rain showers. The food served in cafeterias was so poor they could sometimes not eat it. There were no laundries for washing clothes nor, especially in the early days, women to do it for them. Austin would simply wash both his clothes and his body in the river while some, he said, wore their clothes as long as they could stand it then threw them away and bought new ones. The men confronted malaria—and some became deaf from taking quinine every day. They suffered through poorly trained nurses and doctors, and "indeed many went to an early grave because of the lack of proper care and trained attendants." Particularly in the early years, it was a predominantly homosocial world and the men found life without women to be challenging. "There were many men who didn't seem as though they could get along without the opposite sex."

After a while Harrigan Austin left carpentry and went to work in the heart of the construction project, helping drill for the dynamite explosions that blasted away the Continental Divide in Culebra Cut. "Day and night, sun or rain for they were times when it was compulsory to go through the rain in order not to hold up the shovels or the trains things had to be on time." This was one of the most dangerous jobs. Workers had to run to miss steam shovels headed their way and hope the dynamite they tamped down would not explode prematurely. Austin related working in water up to his waist or watching as rocks or trees fell and crushed the workingmen. Amid all these dangers, the workers felt vulnerable, unsafe, and exploited. Like other workers, Austin compared their situation in the zone to that of a slave—or a soldier fighting in a big war.

Yet Austin took care to comment on the "bright side" of the picture as well, perhaps realizing that too grim a portrait might not win him first prize in the competition. If in the beginning the towns and cities along the line were miserably filthy, with the worst sanitation he had ever seen, conditions did improve over time. Men started bringing their wives and children. Austin began to see better doctors, better food, more justice in the courts, better treatment by superiors, and once churches had been established, "the Isthmus of Panama became a place to be desired." Some men stuck to the job and worked hard—especially, he noted, the West Indians and some of the Europeans. The engineers used dirt and stones to fill in some of the low swamps. Then came the engineering that built the gigantic gates. Many people feared this great project would never succeed. "But Thank God, the Canal has been finished and has become a blessing to the world at large. A great accomplishment, the work of a Great Nation—May God Bless America."

Men like Harrigan Austin encountered in the Canal Zone one of the most industrialized and regimented regions in the world, but they also faced a new world of danger—from disease to premature dynamite explosions and railroad accidents. They struggled to improve their lives by finding a safer job or a kinder foreman. Tracing the writers of Box 25 as they labored to build the Panama Canal allows us to consider how they compared to the workforce as a whole. In their islands of origin, the jobs they did, their level of skill, and their literacy, were they a typical group of workers? The answer, we will see, is both yes and no.

The rising power of the United States would have been visible to Caribbean labor migrants as soon as they stepped foot on the Isthmus of Panama, well before they experienced its authoritarian discipline. Since its victory against Spain in the War of 1898, the force of the United States had become manifested across the Caribbean and Central America. Its military positioned on islands across the Caribbean, the United States intervened powerfully in the political and social structures of Cuba, Puerto Rico, Haiti, and the Dominican Republic. The phenomenal economic and political might of the young nation could be seen across the region via road and railroad construction projects, American citizens purchasing sugar plantations, and United Fruit

32-S-6 Culebra Cut- Cucaracha slide. Looking north from 95 ft level,
showing laborers excavating a ditch through toe of slide. Oct. 11, 1913.

FIGURE 3.1 Workers excavating a ditch after Cucaracha Slide at Culebra Cut, 1913,
National Archives

Company officials increasingly enjoying the spread of their banana plantations across the land.[2]

The US construction project created a canal, nearly fifty miles in length, that raised ships up above the ocean through a series of locks, then sent them through the largest human-made lake in the world at that time, and then down through a second set of locks. The Panama Canal was designed to shine as the brightest beacon of America's ascendant power. It symbolized not only the astonishing ambition of the young country but also its technological and industrial might, its managerial expertise, its scientific and medical mastery, and its ability to create a civilization worthy of white men in the depths of the tropics. In the 1880s the French had tried to build a canal but had failed in devastating fashion. The ignominy of the French effort, it turned out, created a brilliant platform for the effort of US officials. It allowed them to cast their construction project as entirely superior to that of the Old World.

In 1904 a small team of US surveyors, geographers, engineers, doctors, and nurses began their work in the Canal Zone. Conquering the diseases that had done so much to bring down the French canal effort was the first major challenge. Army doctor William Gorgas, who had spent decades in military medicine, most recently in Cuba, was appointed to head the sanitation effort on the Isthmus of Panama. While in Cuba, research by Walter Reed and Carlos Finlay had shown that mosquitos spread both yellow fever and malaria, and Gorgas helped develop sanitation measures to eliminate disease. In his essay "The Conquest of the Tropics for the White Race," Gorgas outlined the policies he implemented in Panama: draining stagnant water or coating it with petroleum, cutting of bushes and grass, placing algaecide in streams, and covering windows with screens (at least in homes of white Americans). Sanitation officials deployed the same measures in Colón and Panama City but went the further step of paving roads and sidewalks and building sewers and waterlines. Officials went door-to-door throughout these cities searching for mosquitos or illness. When they found the former, they fumigated. Throughout 1904, cases of yellow fever and malaria, along with bubonic plague and pneumonia, continued to climb. Workers and officials alike—and their families—sought to return home as anxiety grew about disease. Bureaucratic red tape impeded efforts to build steady momentum. But by the end of 1905, Gorgas's measures took effect and finally conquered yellow fever. Malaria and pneumonia also declined, although they would never be fully eradicated. West Indians would suffer from both diseases throughout the construction period.[3] By early 1906, though, the United States was on its way to a thorough transformation of the vast area it now controlled, the Panama Canal Zone that cut through the heart of the Republic of Panama.

A new and more effective chief engineer, John Stevens, joined the project late in 1905, and he redesigned key elements of the engineering project. The dirt began to fly in the center of the canal's chasm. By the end of that year, thousands of working men and women were contributing to the construction project, and a vast infrastructure had sprung up to support them—from dormitories and houses to cafeterias, hospitals, police stations, prisons, YMCA clubhouses, and baseball diamonds. The workers came from dozens of different countries. Thousands were white US citizens, ready to manage the project, oversee the labor, and fill highly skilled positions as steam shovel engineers, machinists, electricians, carpenters, and the like. The United States also recruited several thousand southern Europeans—most often Spaniards, but also Italians and Greeks—as unskilled laborers, in part to compete with and goad the Afro-Caribbeans to work harder. The latter dominated the workforce—Jamaicans and Barbadians above all, but also men and women from smaller islands of the Caribbean like Grenada, Trinidad, St. Lucia, and Antigua. As Joan Flores-Villalobos has shown in *Silver Women*, the vast majority of Afro-Caribbean women on the Isthmus of Panama came on their own, not as contracted workers for the Isthmian Canal Commission (ICC). They came to live with and support their male partners, or for reasons like those of male workers—seeking better paying jobs, or adventure, or liberation from the brutal colonialism on their home islands. They worked as laundresses or domestic servants most often, and negotiated lives for themselves that were somewhat flexible, balancing between the authority of the US and Panamanian governments and the alternative economy in which they worked.[4]

It is difficult to exaggerate the complexity of the task that lay before the US officials and their workers. Although the French government had made some progress in moving earth, the vast majority of digging and shoveling remained to be done. The United States replaced the original railroad tracks with a new, wider-gauge system. Chief engineer John Stevens redesigned the project to rely on locks rather than a sea-level canal. As a railroad engineer himself, Stevens realized trains would be more central to the job than the French could have imagined. Trains carried workingmen to and from the dig site, and they moved the dirt and rocks away from the construction site. Those materials were then used to build up land areas, helping to create the town of Balboa, for example, that would soon become the headquarters for the canal administration, and building a causeway that stretched out beyond

Panama City and into the sea. The United States was under pressure to shovel away 96 million cubic yards of earth, prevent landslides and avalanches from destroying the work, build lock gates and seaways, and complete the project within a limited schedule and budget. Simultaneously officials needed to manage a workforce of men and women from many different parts of the world, whose numbers grew as high as 45,000 by the time official construction ended in 1914.[5]

In addition, over the years the towns of the Canal Zone expanded as workers' family members joined them, or as children were born on the isthmus. By the end of the construction decade several thousand white US housewives and children had moved to be with their husbands and fathers. Thousands of Caribbean women had likewise traveled to the Canal Zone to be with loved ones and to find work as laundresses, cooks, and domestic servants. According to the Canal Zone Census of 1912, more than 8,500 women of African descent resided there, most of them from Jamaica, Barbados, or Panama. Approximately 2,000 of those were girls aged 14 or younger. Thousands more women, boys, and girls of African descent lived in the Republic of Panama.[6]

To achieve its ambitious goals, the United States needed to manage a diverse and disparate workforce, discipline workers, and maintain order in the boisterous communities across the Canal Zone. In 1907, with chief engineer John Stevens unhappy on the job, a frustrated President Theodore Roosevelt brought army man George Washington Goethals onto the project. Goethals believed the primary challenge involved neither construction nor engineering since "known principles and methods" would be available for those. Raising and managing a large labor force from all over the world—and, increasingly, workers' families as well—constituted the central task. As Goethals saw it, "a novel problem in government was presented by the necessity of ruling and preserving order in the Canal Zone."[7] Solving this constituted, in his eyes, his greatest achievement. Goethals would oversee the construction project, from the building of the enormous lock gates, Gatun Dam, and the flooding of Gatun Lake, to the passage through the canal of the first ship in 1914, and then the depopulation of the zone and elimination of many of its towns upon completion of the project.[8] He would also "rule over" the Canal Zone, developing a highly authoritarian and regimented approach to managing life and labor.

Presidential executive orders buttressed Goethals's power. They stripped the ICC of its authority and gave him complete power in the Canal Zone, answering only to President Roosevelt. The result, as Goethals later described it, was "an autocratic form of government."[9] Anyone, including US citizens, who caused trouble (from mere public disorder to insurrection) or failed to engage in productive labor could be deported from the zone. In no other site controlled by the United States did such broad powers of deportation exist. When warned that these broad powers violated the Bill of Rights, Congress decided to turn a blind eye. In addition, the United States passed sweeping vagrancy laws, arresting and imprisoning men for loitering, vagrancy, intoxication, or disorderly conduct. Time in the penitentiary awaited those who too often violated these laws.[10] A large police force and a team of labor spies maintained order among the workforce, while vagrancy laws subjected men to arrest and the possibility of a prison term if they failed to work as expected or if found intoxicated. Officials enforced those laws vigorously. Union organizers and strikers often found themselves deported. Officials built a penitentiary and put convicts to work building roads in support of the construction project.[11]

As we've seen, the central dynamic of labor control and surveillance in the Canal Zone involved racial and ethnic segregation: due to the "silver and gold" dual payroll system, for the several thousand gold workers, most of them white US citizens, life in the zone was far superior to what they would experience in the United States. They earned higher pay than they would for similar work at home, lived in capacious houses, received six weeks paid vacation and one month paid sick leave each year, and free train travel once a month. The government also developed a suite of recreational activities for white US citizens, from nice hotels and cafeterias to YMCA clubhouses with reading rooms, pool tables, bowling alleys, and gymnasiums, plus baseball leagues and musical and vaudeville acts. All these leisure activities and the clubhouses excluded silver workers. Silver workers, most of whom were West Indians, were paid far less, lived in ramshackle housing with no screens on windows, and ate unappetizing meals with no place provided for sitting during meals.[12]

The Caribbean workforce for the project reached as high as 30,000 or more at a time; over the course of the construction decade 150,000 to 200,000 men and women migrated to the isthmus to support the work. As we trace the writers of Box 25 and their experiences on the isthmus, we might consider how representative these 112 men and women were of the broader workforce. The testimony writers came most often from Barbados and Jamaica, just like the broader workforce. Thirty-eight hailed from Barbados, and twenty-three from Jamaica. I found personnel records on most of the 112 writers; of those twenty-three came from Jamaica, thirty-eight from Barbados, eleven from

FIGURE 3.2 Mealtime at an ICC kitchen for West Indian workers, National Archives

Panama, and the remainder from smaller islands of the Caribbean or other Latin American countries. The Afro-Panamanian workers were likely the children of Caribbean canal workers who had worked on the French construction project and then remained in Panama. Four workers came from Antigua, three each from Grenada and St. Vincent, and two each from St. Lucia and Colombia. One of the Box 25 writers came from each of the following: Martinique, Dominica, French Guiana, British Guiana, Guadeloupe, Montserrat, Trinidad, the Bahamas, Nicaragua, and Honduras. The working men and women in Box 25 also reflect the larger workforce in terms of their ages. Those we're able to trace were in their late teens or early twenties when they migrated to the zone. This was overall a generation of men and women who had been born in the late 1880s to mid-1890s. Those who grew up in Panama often began working at a younger age, like Constantine Parkinson who got a job as a flagman on a survey gang at the age of fifteen.

FIGURE 3.3 Typical housing for West Indian workers, National Archives

Almost all of the 112 writers in Box 25 provided their current address, and most of those still lived in the Republic of Panama or (less often) in the Canal Zone at the time of submitting their entries. Most lived in Panama City, Balboa, Cristobal, Colón—all towns near the canal—or in a few cases they lived farther away in the interior mountains of the Republic of Panama. Only about 10 percent gave their current address as somewhere beyond Panama; of those, five listed their address as a town or city in Jamaica, and the others listed addresses or post office boxes in Antigua, Grenada, St. Lucia, St. Vincent, and Honduras. Although the Isthmian Historical Society advertised widely across the Caribbean and Central America, those who saw the announcements and responded were disproportionally men who had not only migrated to Panama to work on the canal but had remained there the rest of their lives. By contrast, the vast majority of the men and women who worked on the construction project departed the isthmus upon its completion. Some worked a year or two and then headed home or onward to plantations in Cuba,

Honduras, or Costa Rica. Others lasted longer on the construction project but departed as the work wound down in 1914. Those who could save enough money often migrated to the United States, and their demographic flows established the first significant Caribbean community there. These onward migrations constitute one of the most striking aspects of the Panama Canal construction, for they remade the landscape of the Americas and contributed further to making Caribbeans a remarkably cosmopolitan and well-traveled group of people.

In other words, workers who built the canal became part of a vast diaspora spread across Central America, the Caribbean, and the United States. Clearly the ads sent out by the historical society were less successful in generating responses from the islands of the Caribbean than in Panama and the Canal Zone. For that matter, they did not advertise at all in New York City. A sample of veterans of the canal project based in the United States, or even focused more on Barbados or Jamaica, would likely have generated very different discussions, more focused on property accumulation, family migration, and generational wealth.

In the last years of the construction project there was a chaotic mass exodus. Officials struggled to find work for their employees and encouraged them to leave, contacting banana and sugar planters across the region to ask if they needed workers. Although a great many workers ultimately requested repatriation and returned to their home islands, many others stayed. Despite the dangerous aspects of work in the Canal Zone, the US government paid significantly more than workers could make on their home islands or on the banana plantations of Panama or Costa Rica. Many workers flooded into Panama City and Colón, trying to find work or hustling to keep their jobs with the ICC. But by 1920, with the canal fully operable and the landslides under control, only a few thousand workers would be needed to administer and maintain it—instead of the 40,000 or so workingmen employed at the height of the construction period. And many of those would be white-collar workers or skilled white American workers, so permanent jobs for Caribbeans were not easy to find. The writers in Box 25 were among the few who made Panama their permanent home thanks to keeping a job on the Americans' canal. This alone makes them an atypical group. Those who responded to the historical society advertisement were disproportionately men who had spent forty or fifty years after construction ended in canal jobs with the US government. They lived their lives as residents of the Republic of Panama or in the Canal Zone. Those who made their home in Colón or Chorillo confronted the challenges of being Afro-Caribbean in a country shaped by anti-Black racism and xenophobia. And for all of them, the authority of the United States and its white officials had been part of their lives for many years.

British Caribbeans as a group possessed a high literacy rate in the early twentieth century, and migrant British Caribbeans even more so.[13] This is true of those who wrote the testimonies in Box 25 as well. Very few of the entries in Box 25 were apparently written by someone else, and when that was the case, it was more likely due to the infirmity of old age rather than a lack of literacy. The personnel records for silver workers note whether the individual could read and write, and in virtually every case, the Box 25 authors could. Examining hundreds of other personnel records reveals the same result. Indeed, British Caribbeans may be one of the most educated groups of migrant workers in modern history. The British Empire's educational system benefitted those who decided to migrate.[14]

Occupational mobility was one of the trademarks of Panama Canal silver workers, and the testimonies provide ample evidence of this key strategy. For workers living amid a highly regimented, bureaucratic, and authoritarian regime, where refusal to work could result in imprisonment and exploitative working conditions were common, the ability to change jobs was one of the few resources workers could rely upon. And so they did. They acquired skills and moved up to better jobs, they kept the same occupation but moved to an area with a kinder foreman, or they shifted to a different occupation that would pay more money. Mitchell Berisford, who arrived from Barbados in 1909, found work as a waterboy, perhaps the lowest-paying job one could get (seven cents per hour), but moved quickly on to work peeling potatoes in the kitchen. He couldn't bear the smells there, so he got a job as a yard boy, carrying reports to the engineers. In that job, the mud and water destroyed his shoes, so after a couple weeks Berisford joined dockworkers for a short time. Then he moved on again to become a water boy in the timber yard at Cristobal. One day, the foreman watched him help another man in the timber yard, said "you are a good little workman," and offered him a job as a carpenter's helper. His pay rose to thirteen cents per hour. He worked for the next several decades as a carpenter, but along the way shifted from one foreman or work site many times to locate the best conditions and treatment by superiors.[15]

When most people think of the work West Indians did during the canal construction project, they imagine diggers and shovelers—classic unskilled labor. But in fact, the spectrum of jobs held by Caribbeans was much more diverse than that. At the top of the occupational hierarchy for West Indians stood a few hundred white-collar employees: policemen, teachers, store-keepers, and clerical workers. Just below them were skilled workers engaged in craft work, referred to by officials as artisans (officials used this term only for Afro-Caribbean craft workers): electricians, painters, plumbers, carpenters, blacksmiths, boilermakers, molders, pipe fitters, firemen, brakemen, and similar crafts. Earning slightly less pay were "artisan helpers" who assisted the men in the various crafts and who, with luck, might well rise to become artisans themselves. Below them stood the unskilled workers of the oft-imagined West Indian: the "pick and shovel" men who dug away at Culebra Cut, stuffed holes with dynamite, and built roads. Finally, at the lowest occupational level were young boys or older, often injured, men who worked as waterboys or messengers. The pay these men earned varied widely as well, from five cents per hour at the lowest level, to ten cents for pick and shovel men, thirteen cents for artisan helpers, sixteen to twenty cents for most artisans, and twenty-five cents or more for artisans who possessed the most skills. Further complicating the occupational hierarchy was the fact that several thousand workers were paid a monthly salary rather than an hourly wage. The monthly pay was intended for workers whose hours of work were irregular, and workers thus categorized ranged from highly skilled to unskilled. White-collar employees, such as teachers and policemen, earned their pay as a monthly salary, but gravediggers did as well, for example. Railroad workers and boatmen, common silver worker occupations that involved skill, also received a monthly salary.[16]

The occupational hierarchy also shifted over time. In the early years those holding the lowest, most unskilled positions dominated the male Caribbean workforce. Over time, however, the number of artisans and artisan helpers expanded significantly, particularly as the construction project headed toward completion. This occurred in part because the technical requirements of the project shifted over time as less digging and dynamiting was needed. But more importantly, the shift derived from deliberate official policy to replace highly paid white US skilled workers with cheaper West Indians. In August 1909, for example, the ICC employed 5,128 Afro-Caribbean workers paid monthly, 3,646 Afro-Caribbean artisans, and 9,699 Afro-Caribbean laborers. By September of 1914, the number of Afro-Caribbeans paid a monthly salary had increased slightly to 6,334 workers, but the number of artisans had mushroomed to 10,315, and the number of laborers had decreased to 8,038. By this point the skilled labor on the zone was actually dominated by Afro-Caribbeans rather than white US workers, since the total number of gold payroll workers was only 4,712 (a figure that included many white-collar employees as well as skilled mechanics). The occupational categories among Caribbean workers would continue to shift: artisans increased in number as laborers decreased in the following years. In addition, a growing number of laborers were gradually working as artisan helpers and thus deploying some degree of skill.[17]

The men in Box 25 reflect these larger trends in workforce composition. Many of them describe starting out as relatively unskilled workers, as water boys or messengers, or diggers and dynamiters. George Martin arrived on the isthmus and worked with a shovel and pick. Isaias Antioco De La Rosa began as a water boy before moving on to work with a pick and shovel, and then broke rocks to support a road construction project. But while many began in humble positions, the vast majority rose to skilled positions—indeed, a higher proportion achieved skilled jobs than did the workforce as a whole, and so they were outliers in this sense as well. Leonard Chase got a first job loading freight cars with stones, moved on to shifting tracks, then worked his way up to a position as fireman with the railroad. Jamaican Robert Chambers won a job as waiter at Gorgona Hotel, but "the conditions didn't suit me." He changed to a job shifting tracks but found that too difficult, involving as it did working in the rain and mud or jumping out of the way as a train advanced. When he learned of work as a night watchman for the railroad, he quickly took it and then, a few years later, found work as a porter and kept that job for decades until his retirement. Joseph Gard arrived from Barbados in 1906 and began working at the dump, came down with malaria and when released from the hospital found a job at Culebra hotel. In the years to come he moved on to work as a painter, a brakeman, kitchen helper, janitor, fireman, night watchman, and machinist helper. Aaron Clarke found work with the sanitary division, digging ditches and graves. When he could, Clarke would add a few words of prayer before shoveling dirt into a grave. With so much death around them, it is striking that the men had nothing more to rely on than a gravedigger taking time to say a few words as they were laid to rest.

However humbly they began, most of these men moved into jobs that paid better wages. They were distinctly *not* the diggers and dynamiters many people conjure when imagining Afro-Caribbean workers in the Canal Zone. Only ten listed their occupation as laborer. Carpenter and carpenter's helper were the single most common occupations among the 112 men and women, but there were strong constituencies in the skilled trades of the Panama Railroad (brakemen, firemen, switchmen, conductors), several seamen and boatmen, and other industrial trades like blacksmith helper and pipefitter. White-collar (or pink-collar) occupations were well represented, including clerks, telephone operators, salesmen, hospital attendants, waiters, stewards, and cooks. Most of those who responded to the competition had lived in Panama for decades after construction ended, and they had made their way into skilled occupations. Unskilled work was most often phased out as the canal's opening date neared, and it became even less needed once the canal opened to traffic. Unskilled workers thus became the most expendable and typically moved on to other jobs, often in other countries.

These men's lives, in short, like the workforce as a whole, were shaped by remarkable occupational mobility. They changed jobs rapidly and repeatedly. They wanted to get away from cruel foremen or rough working conditions; they moved indoors to get away from massive downpouring rain, or they looked for jobs outside when they hated the smells in kitchens or hospitals. They wanted to be closer to where they lived, or to work alongside family members, or to get away from troublesome neighbors. Most of all they wanted better work and higher pay. The testimonies in Box 25 detail a blizzard of jobs. Constantine Parkinson, in just the four years between beginning work and losing his leg in a train accident, shifted from work as rear flagman in a survey gang to water boy, chainman on a survey gang, promotion to foreman, then finally a more skilled position as brakeman for the Panama Railroad. Unfortunately, that better job also brought with it significant risk: railroad workers were among those most commonly injured. And so it was for Parkinson, who fell victim soon after winning this better job to the accident that cost him his leg. Isaiah Bunting began work at the age of nineteen on the Gamboa Highway and then there followed a lengthy list of occupations: foundry work in the Gorgona machine shop, molder's helper, work carrying hot metal until he got burnt and ended up in the hospital, Colón machine shop until they lowered wages, and then, "I started to run and run around." He tried work on a lemon plantation, then inside for kitchen work, back outside to drive a tractor, and then a job running an electric pump. The list continues with dozens more jobs.

George Peters, likewise, arrived in 1908 from the island of Dominica. He got unskilled work in the steam shovel repair shop at Empire but soon after switched to work helping a mechanic repairing steam shovels out in the dig. There he found the work so rough—the downpouring rain, avalanches, dynamite explosions all around him—that he was pleased to be offered a job as storeman. He switched to driving taxis after a bit, then became a chauffeur. Finally, after the strike of 1920 led to massive firings, he won work as an electrical wireman's helper. It was the best job he'd had yet, and he kept it until retiring thirty-three years later.

These stories remind us of the complex and energetic strategies workers deployed to improve their lives in the Canal Zone. In addition to challenges on the job, workers also had to confront dangers related to the prevalence of disease across the zone. And this also required that they use their wits and creativity to survive.

Because disease had helped destroy French hopes of building the Panama Canal, US officials knew as they arrived on the isthmus in 1904 that overcoming yellow fever and malaria would be critical. Yellow fever remained a killer during the early US occupation of the isthmus. The first chief engineer, John Wallace, brought a metal coffin with him to the isthmus, just as French officials before him had done. Cases of yellow fever appeared every week during that first year, along with bubonic plague, malaria, and pneumonia. Many terrified Americans and Afro-Caribbeans fled for home on the first ships they could find. Yet thanks to the discovery earlier, in Cuba, that mosquitos spread disease, William Gorgas and his medical team effectively eliminated yellow fever by the end of 1905. They destroyed mosquito breeding grounds by draining ditches, spraying oil over standing water, cutting brush, keeping grass cut short, and screening windows. Their teams spread out across Panama City and Colón as well, fumigating, building sewer and water lines, roads, and sidewalks. Gorgas proudly announced that they had eradicated malaria as well as yellow fever. Malaria, however, remained a problem, particularly for Afro-Caribbeans who worked in the swampiest areas and whose shacks typically lacked window screens. In 1906, 821 out of every 1,000 employees were sick with malaria, many of them fatally; gradually the statistics improved until reaching only seventy-six per thousand employees in 1913.[18] Yet other diseases, especially pneumonia, continued to strike men down. As late as 1912, the sanitation department reported that 23,800 Afro-Caribbeans had required treatment either in hospitals or at the "sick camps" or had been reported as sick in their quarters. That statistic means as many as two-thirds of the Caribbean workforce and families were ill during that year, when sanitation measures had supposedly—and officially—made disease a minor problem.[19]

Gorgas argued in 1912 that the two major health problems among Afro-Caribbean workers were pneumonia and liver disease. He attributed the cause of liver disease to excessive consumption of rum, and the pneumonia to Caribbeans' tendency to own only one set of clothing: "They work in the rain all day . . . [and] at night he would go to bed in his wet clothes." Despite this admission by Gorgas, when National Civic Federation reformer Gertrude Beeks visited the zone and urged that measures be taken to help workers remain healthy in the wet conditions (she suggested warming sheds be provided in addition to more blankets, warm showers, and better food), the government argued that none of this was necessary. When Beeks argued that mosquito nets and window screens should be provided to Caribbean workers, chief engineer George Goethals declared that malaria was no longer a problem. Even when it came to pneumonia, Gorgas remained unconcerned. He argued that those falling ill with pneumonia were new arrivals on the isthmus, and he complacently contended that as the number of new workers declined, rates of pneumonia would also fall.[20]

However, the men and women who submitted testimonies to the Isthmian Historical Society competition told a different story. They vividly recalled the threat posed by malaria. Alfred Dottin came to the isthmus on the *SS Ancon* in 1909 and found work as a carpenter at the Pacific terminal. These were no longer the early days, but he nonetheless found conditions difficult. "The working conditions in those days were so horrible it would stagger your imagination. . . . Death was our constant companion. I shall never forget the train loads of dead men being carted away daily, as if they were just so much lumber. Malaria with all its horrible meaning in those days was just a household word. I saw mosquitoes, I say this without fear of exaggerating, by the thousands attack one man. There were days that we could only work a few hours because of the high fever racking our bodies—it was a living hell. Finally typhoid fever got me and I was laid up for 9 weeks in Ancon Hospital hovering between life and death."[21]

George Martin arrived on the isthmus from Barbados in 1909, thinking it was "like a new world." But very soon he learned of the downside: "The fever lashed good and plenty. Sometimes . . . you meet men coming and going in each direction, in a sudden you look, a gang together, something happen, what? One or two of the gang on the ground flatten out, before help reaches, one dead long time, no more of him, thank god." He noted that the ICC officials worked hard to distribute quinine. Some men would throw it out, disliking the bitter taste, but Martin thought it saved him from the disease. All around him, it seemed, were men trying to fight off malaria. "In those days, you watch men shake, gentlemen, you think they would shake to pieces." Hendrix Archbold from Colombia also referenced the year 1909, saying, "I suffered great hardships with malaria fever. The whole place swamped with fever. People were dying daily with Malaria Fever." In 1907–08 so many men were dying the government ran tracks all the way to

Mt. Hope Cemetery to transport corpses efficiently, recalled John Holligan. Allan Belgrave left Barbados for Panama in 1905 and related recurring struggles with malaria as well as dysentery. Upon his discharge from the hospital after recovering from malaria the first time, a doctor warned him, be careful what you eat and don't get wet. "Of course I knew this was impossible, for we had to work in sun and rain." Twelve days after his discharge he landed in the hospital again with malaria and dysentery. This time his doctor took pity and offered him a job in the hospital. "If you go back to work [in Culebra Cut] you won't last very long, so I answered in the affirmative." Rufus Forde said one would head off to work in the morning with 125 men, but by 11:00 A.M. only forty are left, the others "fall down with Malaria." Forde drank quinine as often as he could and credited that with keeping him healthy.[22]

Still, the men feared quinine. In large quantities it could cause side effects from headaches and dizziness to blurred vision or deafness. Barbadian John Prescod remembered "malaria fever have me so bad I hae to drink plenty of quine tonic tell I heard singing in my ears murder murder going to quits drinking quine was getting me deaf." Joseph Gard arrived from Barbados and went to work at Culebra dump. After three weeks he came down with malaria and was sent to a rest house for twelve days. "When I came out I was deaf from the Canine." Harrigan Austin recalled that quinine was prescribed "until many persons couldn't even hear when the engineers blew the engine whistle to get them off the railroad track, and many were killed." St. Lucian Albert Banister, who worked in the boiler shop, never drank alcohol until he got to Panama. "The first gentleman that learn me to drink was Uncle Sammy. . . . When you drink that quinine you feel for 15 minutes you are the sweetest man in the land."[23]

Caribbean men and women also feared the doctors and nurses responsible for keeping them healthy. And they criticized the poor medical care they received, particularly in the early years. There were few doctors and little medicine, one man mentioned. Many Caribbeans felt compelled to rely instead on home remedies. Afro-Caribbeans had reason to take medical advice with a large grain of salt. As we have seen, William Gorgas and other officials were often coldly indifferent to the suffering of Caribbean workers.[24]

The travails of Albert Peters provide a case study in personal struggles with disease as well as the suspicion men felt regarding doctors' care. Peters decided to leave his home in Nassau, Bahamas, in 1906 at the age of twenty-one. His parents had urged him not to go. "They told me about the Yellow

Fever, Malaria, and smallpox that infested the place but I told them that I and my pals are just going to see for ourselves."[25]

Peters arrived on the isthmus with skill as a carpenter, and so he quickly found decent work. But a month after arriving he fell ill with malaria. His stirring story perhaps helped him win first prize in the Isthmian Historical Society's competition. To Peters's surprise, the hospital was merely a row of army tents filled with cots. On his first night there, "the man next to me died and that's the time I remembered my parents plea and wished I had taken their advice." He lived on nothing but quinine for five days and was released, but two weeks later malaria landed him in the tent hospital again. When he caught malaria for a third time, his fever shot to 104 and officials sent him to Colón hospital. The light-skinned Peters was quartered in the European hospital ward with Italians. After three days in the hospital, his fever was worsening. An orderly walked in and ominously placed a screen around his bed. Peters had heard people say that when you are doing poorly the doctors will come and cut you to determine the cause. "As sick as I was I said no operating on me." The orderly returned, stripped him of his pajamas, and laid him on a rubber sheet. "I was stark naked on the sheet, sick but ready for action." The orderly returned, this time with a towel and a basin. Peters, terrified, thought it was ether to put him to sleep so the doctor could operate. As the orderly began to place the towel on his face, "I don't know where I got the strength from, but I drew my two feet up and let him have it in the chest." The orderly fell back against the screen and onto the ground as Peters jumped out of bed to ask what he was doing. A nurse calmed Peters, explaining that they were seeking only to cool him and reduce his fever. "I really thought it was something like ether to put me to sleep until the doctor came to cut, but it was ice water." He apologized. After a few more weeks recovering without further incident, Peters returned to work.

Adding insult to injury, many men felt the authorities cared little about their suffering. James Ashby noted that men might be sick or dying but their bosses still expected them to show up for work. Anyone who refused to work was banned from sleeping in the government camps or might end up in jail. As a result, they often tried to work through their illness. Tales of men suffering through the symptoms of malaria while working at their jobs pervaded in the zone.

Some of the testimony writers, to be sure, expressed gratitude for the care they received. When they did, however, they talked about nurses, not doctors. James Williams arrived in the zone as a young teenager. He worked as a kitchen helper, but the kitchen was alongside the Chagres River with many mosquitos. He soon caught malaria. A doctor inspected him at the kitchen and said "you are going to be sick boy" and instructed him to report to sick camp and tell them to send him to the hospital. "He further asked me, Are you a God fearing man? I replied yes. He said to me you are going to die." Williams described riding the train to Ancon hospital. As he arrived at Panama Station, there stood many horse-drawn ambulances waiting to take patients to the hospital. He was met by a pleasant American nurse who took his pulse and appeared frightened. She told the orderly, "Do not put this patient under the shower, give him a bed bath." The orderly put a heavy waterproof blanket on the bed and then threw buckets of cold water and crushed ice on top of it. Then, Williams related, they had "not even the courtesy as to consult me but stripped me naked and threw me in that cold deadly water. To be truthful, I thought I could not any longer live." The orderly dried him off and the treatment helped his fever, but Williams was "still fretting over that ice bath as I had never heard or seen anything like that before." For days he was given quinine to drink until one morning men came with a stretcher and carried him out of the ward. "I thought they were going to bury me as I was actually given over as dead." It turned out they had discovered he had typhoid fever, not malaria, and were moving him to a different ward.

In the end Williams recovered, and he attributed this in part to the care he received while in the hospital. "What I can truthfully say Those American Nurses my own dear mother could not be more kind and tender to me." He had no desire to eat food—"my life was ebbing out. But how they plead with me to take some nourishment." One night a nurse came to him and said, "Now, Bed 6, if you don't take some nourishment you would never get well and the tone she spoke to me with her hand on my head I forced to swallow a little milk and from that I continued to take little by little and a few days past and she came on at night and took my temperature and said, you are getting better, 'Bed 6.'"[26]

While disease was a constant threat to the health of Caribbean workers, the Box 25 testimonies provide excruciating tales of other dangers as well— landslides, dynamite explosions, train accidents, steam shovels toppling over, and falling from the gigantic lock gates, among others. The zone was an extremely dangerous place to work, particularly if you were an Afro-Caribbean man or woman. Consider the constant train traffic; during the construction decade there were few roads in the zone. Most people traveled either by riding on trains or by walking along train tracks. There were common fatalities when people didn't see or hear a train approaching behind them or when trains crashed or went off the tracks. And in Culebra Cut alone there were several layers of train tracks rising up the mountain side, with trains constantly going back and forth, carrying laborers to the cut or moving the spoils of the dig away. We saw above that Constantine Parkinson lost a leg when working as a brakeman on a train that crashed. Jeremiah Waisome likewise described riding the labor train to work one day. It was going full speed with ten cars full of laborers attached to it. Someone had left a dead-end track open, with train cars parked on it, and Waisome's train crashed into it. Many workers were killed. "One could hear the moaning and hollering, that morning it was awfull. . . . God was with me that morning."[27]

Dynamite explosions were also common causes of injury and death. In the worst recorded accident, in December 1908, 44,000 tons of dynamite exploded and, according to official records, killed twenty-six men and wounded forty-nine. The explosion sent machinery and bodies flying across Culebra Cut. Laborer Amos Clarke remembered it differently from the government tally—he related that the dynamite went off, "blowing to pieces over 300 men. Their instral and flesh could be seen hanging on the faraway trees. It was something awful and horrible to look at." Smoke from the explosion could be seen three miles away. Work on the powder gangs, which set off the dynamite, must have been one of the most dangerous jobs. Edgar Simmons described the experience: "Some of us has up to 65 or 72 holes to light up and find our way out. So, to you sponsors of the Isthmian Historical Society, you can judge the situation, when 9 of us start out, each one with two sticks of fire in our hand, running and lighting, at the same time trying to clair ourselves before the first set begin bursting on us. Then its like Hell. Excuse me of this assertion, but it's a fact." Mitchell Berisford of Barbados described the sight of so many fatalities caused by dynamite explosions, premature or not: "The flesh of men flew in the air like birds many days."[28]

These constant dangers and accidents meant that many men ended their days on the job missing a limb or bearing scars. Others met their death in the Canal Zone. Although the official record stated that only 3,500 Caribbeans died during the construction years, the total was undoubtedly much higher than that. Workers' tendency to change their name and their residency hampered officials' ability to keep adequate records. In addition, precise recording of the number of fatalities was not a high priority for the US government. In any case, the testimonies speak to the constant presence of death, and their fears and anxieties about it, better than any official record. "Death was our constant companion," Alfred Dottin noted. Dottin often saw trainloads of the dead heading to the cemetery at Mt. Hope. Leslie Carmichael recalled that men would often sing the song "Somebody Dying Every Day" while shifting tracks or setting up the dump cars. Death from disease was so common that, as Albert Peters described it, "if you had a friend that you always see and missed him for a week or two, don't wonder, he's either in the hospital or at Monkey Hill [the original name for Mt. Hope Cemetery] resting in peace." And as powerful as the descriptions of death are in the testimonies, the apparent indifference of white US officials and skilled workers comes through with equal clarity. Reginald Beckford, who was born in Colón, told the story of the well-known locomotive engineer Billy, whose policy was "that he wil stop his train on the tracks for a horse, or a cow but not for a human." One day Billy's train went by, and Beckford saw people running to the tracks to see half a man's body lying there. "The train did not stop after running over the man until it reaches Monkey Hill."[29]

For support amid these difficulties, Caribbean workers looked to each other and their own spiritual faith. Amos Parks commented that "the reason we all use to go to church more regular than today, because in those days you see today and tomorrow you are a dead man. You had to pray everyday for God to carry you safe, and bring you back. Those days were horrible days to remember."[30]

The 112 men and women who submitted testimonies for the Isthmian Historical Society competition shared many basic experiences with the broader workforce. Their writings vividly depict the challenges workers faced in the Canal Zone—the premature dynamite explosions and avalanches, the constant threat of death, and the sense that officials cared little for their suffering and treated them with racist condescension. Like other workers, they changed jobs often in order to improve their lives. Yet in important respects, the authors of Box 25 were an atypical group. They were more likely than the average worker to have achieved a skilled job that brought with it higher wages and some authority, and they were among the relatively few workers who remained in Panama or the Canal Zone for the rest of their lives, working for the US government. Their testimonies contest the official governmental record on issues ranging from the prevalence of disease to the hardships of working conditions. Amid the tremendous challenges they faced during the construction years, how did Afro-Caribbeans experience their world and carve an autonomous space for themselves? The testimonies provide clues for answering this question. The next chapter examines how Afro-Caribbeans fought to achieve a modicum of control over their lives amid the highly authoritarian and regimented world of the US Canal Zone.

CHAPTER FOUR

Caribbean Identities

Jules LeCurrieux began his testimony for the competition formally: "For the Societies information I the author of the history of my life spent on the Canal Zone from the 14 of Jan 1906 when arrived here as an emigrant from the island of Barbados BWI." He was born in Cayenne, French Guiana, but moved as a young child with his family to Barbados. At the age of seventeen he boarded a ship in Bridgetown for Panama. His experience on the construction project was, as for so many, challenging. An accident injured his eye, and he was hospitalized and then unable to work for a year. A boss blamed him for an accident when he returned to work and fired him; this same boss (one of the "biggest" in the zone, he said) got LeCurrieux fired from other jobs he had secured. Realizing that he was, in effect, blacklisted, LeCurrieux felt forced to move to a different section of the construction project.

Describing these travails, LeCurrieux's testimony includes a wide range of reflections and tones. At some points he comes across as quite deferential, praising the US government that built the canal: "I thank God with all my heart and may He forever bless the US govt and continuously be her protection." At other times, he strikes a more assertive tone. He relates a labor action he and others conducted. They refused to work on an oil tanker because they smelled oil leakage and knew it was unsafe. The boss demanded: "if you men want to work get back down in the hole." LeCurrieux refused, noting that the boss was staying safe in his office. Later he learned that more obedient men who had gone back down were injured that same day. Along with such confrontations, LeCurrieux described the hardships caused by poor food, constant rain, avalanches, and cruel treatment by foremen. "I am yet alive after seeing with my eyes individuals run over by trains and engines, killed by powder blasts, killed by falling off the locks."

These were the true pioneers who made possible this stunning achievement, he stressed: yet they continued to feel disrespected by the US government who gave them only a pittance in cash relief: "most of us just have to take what we are allowed until those who are in authority some day to reconsider our real needs and distresses, and oblige us with something more decent." He could only hope to live long enough to see that day "when I will rejoice in the labor of my helping hand in the completion of one of the worlds greatest mysteries."[1]

This dizzying blend of reflections in LeCurrieux's essay reminds us that Afro-Caribbean identity was complex and fluid. We see this in historians' portrayal of Afro-Caribbeans as well. The tens of thousands of Afro-Caribbeans who worked to build the Panama Canal are represented in different, even contradictory images. Scholars often present them as downtrodden diggers, exploited by brutal foremen and confronting the constant threat of disease and premature dynamite explosions. In many accounts they seem passive, accepting of their lot, nearly the deferential and gentlemanly stereotype that US officials desired them to be.[2] But as Rhonda Frederick noted in her book *Colón Man A Come*, Afro-Caribbean canal workers cannot be reduced to mere victims of economic exploitation and labor migration. She explores the mythography of the "Colón Man" who "can be identified by his migration-forged masculinity, cocky attitude, material possessions, broadened worldview, and sometimes his work-related illnesses." Such representations of cosmopolitan globetrotters, often created when Caribbean laborers returned home and informed by literary descriptions of their worlds, might show a "Colón Man" strutting down the streets of Kingston or Bridgetown, wearing a long trench coat as was fashionable, perhaps a shark tooth necklace round his neck.[3] This Colón man is savvy, worldly, ready to fight for his place in the world. Examining the testimonies in Box 25 in the context of other primary sources can help reconcile these contradictory images. They suggest both the multiple identities that emerged amid life and work in the zone and the ways Afro-Caribbeans drew upon cultural resources from their home islands and developed new strategies on the Isthmus of Panama.

As Afro-Caribbean canal workers sat down to recount their memories for the competition, they were all facing major life challenges. Recall that the vast majority of writers for the competition resided in Panama or, in a few cases, in the Canal Zone.[4] As we saw in chapter 1, Afro-Caribbean Panamanians in the Republic of Panama confronted a popular and elite politics of xenophobia and nationalism. Even in the 1960s, when the original canal builders were aged men and women, they continued to feel marginalized by the status quo in Panama. They were often in poor health and in most cases faced severe poverty. Most were now in their mid-to-late seventies. They needed help, medically and financially, and it was not going to arrive by normal processes. Some received a small pension from the US government, but many did not. And even that was a small pittance that left recipients feeling impoverished. Thus the promise of prize money was a rare opportunity to improve their quality of life at least for a while.

Many of the writers discussed their health, old age, or lack of money. Alonzo West, who had joined the British West Indies Regiment and then worked on the docks of the Canal Zone until retiring in 1953, asked the historical society to excuse any mistakes in his entry, "for old age takes away remembrance." John Morgan of Colón wrote only a few sentences for the competition, relating some jobs he had held, and then got to his main concern: "I am not getting any pension. I took sick before it start to give out, and up to know I am still sick going 30 years now. I am asking you to see what you can do for me." And St. Lucian Albert Banister wrote, "I am nervus my eyes is weak I remain your sincear faithful servent."[5]

Many authors emphatically praised the United States and expressed their gratitude to the nation. "Praise heaven, to the Americans, for the Panama Canal," wrote George Martin. Berisford Mitchell, who signed his entry as "retiree and vetterant," related several near-death experiences while working on the canal and concluded, "So my dear Sir I have plenty to thank God for that my life is still speared to this day I have plenty to thank the Americans for. I have to say you all are a blessed people a nation which God bless, and to you Sir I hope through my rough toils and my experances of the Panama Canal, that the Lord may send us a blessing for our hard toiling, and that you may see fit to give me one of your prizes." Edward White had arrived in Panama on a sunny afternoon from Westmoreland Parish, Jamaica, a young man of twenty years. He worked at many jobs, like so many other Caribbeans, before landing work at the Ancon laundry and remaining there for twenty-seven years. "Today," he said, "I am a very sick man, stricken with a stroke for almost three years. But I am also a very lucky man. . . . All that you good people have done for us, and are still doing, I am most grateful. The packages of food every month, the doctor's care . . . the medcines and the kind patience with us who are so miserable at times." He ended, "May God never cease to bless America, its Presidents, and its people. May 'He' strengthen you all, and keep you that you will always be able to help us the poor ones, who have to depend solely on the mercy of God, and the goodness of the American People."[6] These writers may have written with utmost sincerity in praising the United States, but they may also have believed it would ingratiate them with the judges and help their chances of winning a prize.

While the kind generosity of these comments and the confession of vulnerability and old age would seem to suggest men eager to please their superiors, other themes of the essays reflect a more critical perspective.

Many contain a critique of US policies as well as a determination to high-light the contributions—even the heroism—of Caribbeans to the project. And they also noted explicitly the tendency of many Americans to discount their achievements. One man, E. W. Martineau, quoted a Panamanian labor union leader as saying the USA "has dumped West Indians in Panama and Colón and made a great problem for us." This, said Martineau, "was not true and did not worth the paper it was written on." According to Amos Parks, "Construction days will never be forgotten by the West Indian People who gave their lives for the digging of the Canal. That's why I always say the younger generation of today whose parents lose their lives they should be recompense greatly."[7]

Sprinkled throughout the essays were comments praising the hard work and skill of Afro-Caribbeans—sometimes to the detriment of other groups, including white and Black Americans, Panamanians, and Europeans. Albert Banister was one of several who credited West Indians with the success of the project. "West Indian lives and blood was taken to put through this canal," he noted; but by comparison, "we had colored Americans good men skillful men but they can't pull with the white Americans always a fight." Enrique Plummer declared that African Americans spent little time in the Canal Zone. Officials sent them home because "they were making trouble." African American men working as teamsters, for example, would refuse to unload the trucks, saying that was not their job. And they were "tutoring" others to behave the same way, he said, so officials got rid of them.[8]

Other writers noted the skill and bravery with which West Indians labored. Visiting the "great Culebra cut," E. W. Martineau saw the "work men cautiously creeping up the ridges with their drills as soldiers going up Majuba Hill in Mesopotamia, in battle array. With great dexterity they pressed forward in blasting and drilling, while others with water hose washing down the soft earth to make way for the gallant men who were storming the rocks with gallantry." Prince George Green explained, "You see most of us came here with the same spirit as a Soldier going to war, dont dodge from work or we will never finish it, and it was done not in Six days, but our part was completed, thank God, I live to see the foundation we have laid down. become a living Paradise for those who are enjoying life to its heights on the Canal Zone today, while us who labored as hard as hell to help compete it can only pass through and look at it and Say I have worked here and there in the Construction of the Canal."[9] Several of the men carefully noted the various skills they had developed—whether their white supervisors allowed them to make use of those skills was a different matter. But the most common aspiration expressed in the testimonies was simply to note the great contributions they and other West Indians made to the building of the canal. The Pan-Afro-Caribbean consciousness that scholars have detected in later decades likely had its origins in the common challenges islanders confronted in the Canal Zone during these early years.

Caribbean men and women faced not only the dangers of the construction project and rampant disease but also the overwhelming power of the US government bureaucracy and its many rules and regulations. In a world that sought to reduce them to tools of production, Caribbean men nonetheless shaped identities that claimed their right to pride in their own labor and skills, that saw and named the racism of US officials, and that called upon their heritage as subjects of the British Empire as a source of strength.

Consider first how Caribbeans saw their American bosses. Edgar Llewelyn Simmons (aka "Shine"), whom we met in the introduction, had a simple way to refer to the US men all around him: the white faces. His first morning on the isthmus, Simmons was awakened at 6:00 A.M., told to line up, and then "we turn out only to meet some white faces again." Many of the other testimonies in Box 25 discuss and describe the whiteness that surrounded them. George Martin had been a carpenter at home in Barbados, but in the zone his first job was with a shovel and pick. Describing the constant rain that shaped their workdays, he said, "It turned us colored people almost white, but our boss, it brought him like white Calico, I mean white." Repeatedly throughout the testimonies, workers make distinctions based on race: white bosses versus the colored or Black fellows working alongside them.[10]

It is not surprising that Caribbean workers focused on racial differences. The pervasive structure of the gold and silver payrolls meant that every individual's status and identity was profoundly connected to race. The gold payroll focused on white US workers who were paid in gold and received the best housing, paid vacations, pleasant cafeterias, and YMCA clubhouses for their leisure time. Being on the silver payroll meant not only that Afro-Caribbeans received their pay in silver but also that they faced exclusion from the clubhouses and cafeterias for white men, and they lived in rough housing that lacked window screens and other niceties. Because of the silver and gold system, racial and ethnic distinctions shaped even the most intimate aspects of life in the zone. In the eyes of US officials, the tens of thousands of men from Barbados, Jamaica, Grenada, St. Lucia, and other islands were to be managed and disciplined as efficiently as possible. They had settled upon Caribbeans as their major source of labor for many reasons, chief among them the perception that Antilleans were "harmless and law-abiding," childlike, and easily controlled. That Jamaican laborers had worked well, overall, during the 1880s French construction effort, and that they spoke English was an added benefit.[11] Yet these essential workers were also young, exhausted men who found conditions in the new industrial empire extremely difficult. Officials understood relatively little about the distinctive cultures Caribbeans brought to their work—how a St. Lucian man, for example, might differ from an Antiguan, and why both might have reason to feel suspicious of a Jamaican supervisor. Instead, officials lumped all Caribbean workers together as West Indian.

The 112 men and women in Box 25 understood how they were perceived by US officials. Rufus Lucas described working as an oiler in the dredging division. One day his boss unexpectedly fired him. "It was for no just cause but I couldn't talk back because in those days every white man thought he was GOD down here." They repeatedly complained of feeling treated like animals. Jules LeCurrieux wrote about his shock upon arriving in the Canal Zone. "To our surprise we were loaded off the trains as animals and not men, and almost under strict guard to camps, and in some sections to canvas tents." Constantine Parkinson likewise described the death that surrounded their lives. "In construction days people get kill and injure almost every day and all the boses want is to get the canal build."[12]

Many others wrote about the racism they experienced while working for the US government. "In the early days," noted E.W. Martineau, "these men were very discriminative, they disliked any individual who was not of Caucasian blood." He heard a judge say that "one policeman's word is as good as 10 civilian's word in his court." A striking story in this regard came from Jeremiah Waisome, the young man born in Nicaragua whom we met in the introduction. As a schoolboy on the isthmus, at the age of twelve, Waisome could no longer bear seeing friends with their pockets full of Panamanian silver balboas on payday. He slipped away without his mother's knowledge and approached a man in Balboa for a job as a water boy. The boss was chewing a big wad of tobacco and he said, yes, I need a water boy. Waisome noticed that the man had written his name down incorrectly. "So I said excuse me boss my name do not spell that way, he gave me a cow look, and spit a big splash, and look back at me and said you little nigger you need a job, I said yes sir, he said you never try to dictate to a white man, take that bucket . . . and bring water for those men over there." Waisome's story undoubtedly described a typical experience. Harrigan Austin summed up the lesson Black Caribbeans learned: "To some degree life was some sort of semi slavery, and there was none to appeal to, for we were strangers and actually compelled to accept what we got . . . and the bosses or policemen or other officials right or wrong could be always wining the game."[13]

In some ways, their situation—the feeling of "semi slavery" as Austin put it—surely seemed familiar to Caribbeans accustomed to British colonialism and the stranglehold over the economy held by the planter elite. In both old and new worlds, white men and women ruled over them, as they saw it, like slave drivers. Eric Walrond, the Trinidadian author who wrote so eloquently of Panama, portrayed a West Indian mother in the Canal Zone scolding her aimless son in his short story "Panama Gold": You must work, she declared, because otherwise where will I get any food? She admonished him to accept the authority of his foreman, using the Jamaican patois term for a white man in authority and rooted originally in slave relations: "Boy yo' bes' mek up yo' min' an' get under de heel o' de backra."[14] As in Barbados or Jamaica, workers found that organized, mass protests were difficult or impossible to launch. The new stranglehold they faced stemmed from the infinite authority of US officials, who could deport or imprison anyone deemed troublesome or unproductive. Officials also maintained a vast surplus of Caribbean workers and made a point of bringing more men from diverse islands and from Spain, Italy, and Greece in order to manage and control them more easily. Together these conditions forced workers either to accommodate themselves to the harsh regime or develop hidden forms of resistance.

Indeed, officials' reliance on a vast surplus provides one indication that Afro-Caribbeans asserted themselves when they could. In the earliest, most chaotic and disease-ridden days of construction, the first and final act of rebellion for some workers involved a lesson learned back on their home islands, when slaves fled into the hills or plantation workers feigned illness to avoid work: many simply jumped back onto a ship and fled for home. In later years, the typical work pace was so intense that workers routinely stayed away from the job, particularly on rainy days or when they had earned enough money to get by for a while. Some workers went beyond taking a break for a day or two to slip away to their home island for a visit. Engineer D. D. Gaillard, who oversaw the work on Culebra Cut, noted that he had to keep a workforce of 14,000 men in order to ensure he would have at least 10,000 show up on any given day.[15]

Workers also resisted by eluding the constant control and surveillance of US authorities, and here again they surely drew upon strategies developed after emancipation to elude colonial control. Dissatisfaction with the quality and price of food in government cafeterias generated a mass exodus out

23-1

THE PANAMA CANAL
APPLICATION FOR PHOTO-METAL CHECK—EMPLOYEES
(Typewrite or write very plainly)

FILE No.

MR 63592

Cristobal, C. Z., Dec. 17, 191 8

To EXECUTIVE SECRETARY (through Head of Division):

Name......J. W. Wasom...... Gold Roll / Silver Roll } Check No. { Photo-Metal 32188 / Present 163952

Division......P. R. R. Supt's...... Gang No...1268

Occupation......Chauffeur...... , at { ------ cts. per hour / $ 55.00 per month

Employed, effective...................., 191.. to take the place of......
(For new employees only)

In present rating since................, 191.. His service is required on account of......
(Date) (New employees only)

Previously employed in The Panama Canal service or by the Panama Railroad Company?...Yes
(Yes or No)

Citizen of...South American...... Date of birth...July 24, 1895... Place of birth...Nicaragua, S. A.
(Give month, day, and year)

Post office address......Cristobal, C. Z....... Isthmian residence...Colon, R. P.

Arrived on Isthmus......Aug. 3, 1896...... Married, single, divorced, or widowed
(Cross out those not applicable.)

Color...Black......
(White, black, brown) Able to read and write?...Yes... Able to sign name?...Yes

Sex Male / Female Height...5...ft. 11...in. Weight...132...lbs.

Physical deformities or peculiarities, such as scars, moles, and missing members?

None

(FOR GOLD EMPLOYEES ONLY—CIRCLE DESCRIPTION APPLICABLE)
Color of eyes: Blue, chestnut, greenish maroon, maroon, dark maroon, yellow, brown, gray.
Color of hair: Black, blond, chestnut, gray, red, white. BALD
Kind of hair: Straight, wavy, curly, kinky.

Where employed......Cristobal Coaling Station...... Restricted areas required to enter on

official business......

Approved and forwarded:

CW Morgan
(Head of Division.) O. K. (Foreman.) (Signature of employee.)

(FOR USE OF OFFICIAL PHOTOGRAPHER ONLY)

Balboa / Cristobal Studio

Photograph taken...................... Plate No......9146

Emergency permit................issued. Initials......

Completed and forwarded to Identification Office......APR 16 1919...... Initials......

Recorded and forwarded to applicant...................... Initials......

Emergency permit returned and filed......

NOTE.—Two copies of this form must be filled out for each employee. Forms for gold employees required to enter the locks, electric or water supply plants, must be forwarded to the Executive Secretary after approval by head of division. Forms for all other employees will be delivered in person by the employee to the Official Photographer, after approval by head of division. FINGER PRINT IMPRESSIONS WILL BE TAKEN BY OFFICIAL PHOTOGRAPHER.

FIGURE 4.1 Jeremiah Waisome's application for photo-metal check, National Personnel Records Center

of government housing. Rent outside the US-controlled zone, in Panama City or Colón, was terribly high, yet most Antillean workers preferred either moving to those cities or making a home for themselves in the Panamanian bush. And although officials quickly responded by ending the requirement that employees purchase meal tickets, the number of residents in government housing never rebounded. Living on their own not only meant they could cook for themselves, it also meant freedom from much of the government's surveillance and harsh discipline, including roundups and possible imprisonment for skipping a day of work.[16]

US officials tended to see Caribbean workers as a homogenous group, but in fact they followed very different paths in Panama. Because Jamaicans had to pay an emigration tax to leave the island and go to Panama, and because a larger independent peasantry and Black middle class existed on that island, those in the Canal Zone were often more skilled, more likely to possess some resources, and more likely to receive plum jobs as teachers, policemen, foremen, or skilled workers. As a result, Jamaicans were often feared or distrusted by other Antilleans. Other Caribbean workers saw them as most likely to support and enforce the US government's authoritarian regime. Over time, the occupational landscape of the Antillean community in the Canal Zone grew more complex as US officials, seeking to save money, began training Caribbeans to do skilled work that had previously been carried out by white US workers. Although still generally referred to as "helpers," kept on the lower-status silver payroll rather than the gold roll (which was reserved for white US workers), and paid far less than white men, these skilled Caribbean workers received training and became carpenters, machinists, plumbers, railroad conductors, firemen, brakemen, and switchmen. Widening job opportunities improved life for many silver employees: their pay increased, their work became easier than that of diggers and dynamiters, and their greater access to resources afforded them more freedom from US government surveillance and control.[17]

Thus the labor hierarchy was far more complex in the Canal Zone than references to a homogenous "West Indian workforce" would suggest. More skilled and/or lighter-skinned workers experienced a different racial climate. Although fewer in number, the testimonies by Central Americans provide evidence of the fluidity of race. Alfonso Suazo, a Nicaraguan who came to the zone as a child by way of Honduras, won third prize for his very long and descriptive entry to the Isthmian Historical Society competition. His father worked in a skilled position, he explained, as a deep-sea diver, and this meant they were given a house next to white families in La Boca.

Unspecified by him was the racial component—it was likely not only his father's socioeconomic status but also the proximity to whiteness of the family, as Central Americans not of African descent—that enabled them to win a residence in a white neighborhood. Yet Suazo, though enjoying some privileges closed off to Afro-Caribbeans, nonetheless noted the brutality of life in the zone. When yellow fever caused many deaths, he noted that workers were instructed to cart the dead off to the cemetery, dumping their bodies into a mass grave—some still alive as they were carried away.[18]

As workers adjusted themselves to the Americans' regime on the Isthmus of Panama, as they confronted the racism, disease, extremely difficult and dangerous working conditions, poor food, and uncomfortable or exploitative housing, they found they had little recourse. It was dangerous at worst and typically futile at best to complain to a supervisor or foreman. Silver employees had no union to represent them. George Washington Goethals, chief engineer of the construction project from 1907 to 1914, opened his office every Sunday morning to any resident or employee who had a grievance, and he hired one full-time inspector to investigate problems and suggest potential remedies. The records of that inspector demonstrate that complaints were indeed investigated, but they also show that most grievances were filed by white US men and women, not silver roll workers. Considering the demographics of the zone, and that the number of Afro-Caribbeans far overwhelmed the number of white US citizens (somewhere above 30,000 for the former versus fewer than 5,000 for the latter), Goethals's grievance system could hardly have been sufficient.[19]

The other recourse for Caribbeans, and one that made a greater impact on their daily lives, kept them entangled in the British Empire even as they toiled for the Americans. Although the United States dominated the zone, diplomatic representatives from the British Empire watched over and reported on the conditions facing tens of thousands of that empire's subjects. The colonial governments of each Caribbean island—from Martinique and Haiti to Barbados, St. Lucia, Grenada, and Jamaica—played a role as well. But the most intense observation and most powerful interventions were provided by the British consul's office. Claude Mallet, the man in charge, had a full-time job representing the subjects of his queen.

Mallet had lived in Panama since 1879 when his father began serving as British consul. He served on the consulate staff for the next forty years, becoming consul himself in 1903 and then minister to Panama and Costa Rica in 1914. Although some West Indians wrote directly to London for help or to inform the diplomatic corps of an injustice, most relied on Consul Mallet.

They informed him of problems ranging from poor food to unsatisfactory housing, mean or racist foremen, bad job assignments, undeserved incarceration, and bad treatment by Panamanian police.[20]

Mallet found all this annoying. That he regarded West Indians as harshly as did any white American can be seen in his response to riots on a United Fruit Company plantation in Limon, Costa Rica, in 1910. Migrants there, originally from St. Kitts, demanded to be repatriated after many of their group had fallen ill and some had died. The United Fruit Company had done little or nothing to help. Mallet deemed their protest "preposterous." He bragged that he had handled many strikes during the French and now the American phases of construction. "What I have always done has been to get the employer to do what is just toward the men and then tell them in unmistakable language to work, and if they do not work they will starve, and that if they disturb public order the government counts upon enough force to keep the peace, and their acts be upon their own heads if they suffer in consequence of defying armed forces."[21]

Mallet himself was a transimperial actor, of course, representative of Anglo-American cooperation and collaboration in the Caribbean and beyond during the early twentieth century. And unfortunately for laborers, Mallet saw the Americans as a vast improvement on the French, who earlier had worked to build the canal, and so he felt little sympathy for British colonial subjects who complained of poor treatment by US officials. In 1906 Mallet wrote to the governor of the Canal Zone that "the conditions of the labouring man in the Canal Zone, as regards his treatment, are better to-day than they have ever been within my recollection." That same year, when President Theodore Roosevelt visited the isthmus he inquired of Mallet how the West Indians were doing. The British consul admitted he had not personally inspected the housing or food provided to laborers, but that "since the negro is quick to bring a grievance to the attention of the Consul . . . at the present time, they were so few and trivial I generally found upon investigation that they had no foundation and therefore was convinced the labourers must be well treated and well cared for by the Commission."[22]

Conditions undoubtedly were better than they had been during the French construction era, but that they were nonetheless problematic is also beyond debate. Socialist member of Parliament J. Keir Hardie wrote the colonial office after hearing complaints about treatment of West Indians. "Surprise is expressed among American officials at the non-interference of the British government." Hardie had no doubt that conditions would improve if the British intervened. British Colonial Office officials required Mallet to report on the matter. Privately they noted they had been right not to promote Mallet to a higher position, suggesting they, like Keir Hardie, saw him as too sympathetic to US officials' way of handling laborers.[23]

When laborers pushed Consul Mallet to provide help, they often emphasized their rights as subjects of the Crown. One man wrote Mallet to ask him to help a friend who had been unjustly imprisoned in Panama. "Sir I am not his Counsil But I am an English subject also I has a great knowledge of this Law I know what you can do from what you cant Therefor I ask you to take a Part of that young man life as I do remember the Laws of England." When Mallet refused to help, many laborers pleaded to their diplomatic representatives in England. One man wrote for help after an accident required amputation of his leg and he had received neither compensation nor even a wooden leg from the US government. "I know that my Mother Court will not forsake these few lines."[24]

In the end, the problem lay not just with Mallet; British officials generally seem to have shared his willingness to see racism in the Canal Zone as inevitable and, perhaps, justified. In 1910 Caribbeans in the zone reacted with horror when a white US citizen killed a West Indian and then was acquitted despite strong evidence against him. The American, Louis Dennison, shot his victim in the heart with no provocation. Mallet noted that West Indians were very upset and believed that the case showed "that a white American can kill a negro with impunity in the Canal Zone." Mallet confessed, "There is certainly good grounds for that belief, and I agree . . . that it is unlikely a jury composed of Canal employees will ever convict a white American and a fellow employee for the murder of a negro." Dennison had confessed to the crime, saying, "I have only killed a nigger, don't be too hard on me boys." British official A. Mitchell Innes, based in Washington, DC, reflected on the incident: "All those who are accustomed to dealing with the evidence of coloured people know how hard it is to obtain from them a consistent, truthful, unvarnished tale, and unless the witnesses have concocted a story beforehand, irreconcilable discrepancies arise which are fatal to the case of the prosecution." A handwritten note added to this one, by someone in the London office of foreign secretary Edward Grey, stressed that Dennison was undoubtedly guilty, yet since he believed West Indians could not be trusted he saw no way to remedy the situation.[25]

The continued ties Afro-Caribbeans felt to their British representatives could be observed when the former needed help. At those times they often stressed their rights as subjects of the British Empire. William J. Karner, the labor recruiter who served briefly as acting chief engineer in the early days of construction, commented on his dislike of the Jamaican laborers. "They are sort of an I.D.W.W. class (I don't want to work unless driven to it). As British subjects, they think they are close to royalty and quite superior to white laborers from the US." When ordered to do something too curtly by a foreman, he related, "The laborer would straighten himself up and say to the foreman, 'I wish you to understand, sir, that I am a British subject, and if we cannot arrange this matter amicably we will talk to our Consul about it.'" Supervisors like Karner undoubtedly found it difficult, amid their assumptions of racial and national superiority over Caribbean laborers, that they had to contend with self-assertion, a fluency with the English language, and even the backing of the British Empire when seeking to order their workers about. Karner concluded, "There is where the man had us at a disadvantage. As a British subject, or 'British object,' as we called him, he knew that his government was back of him and would protect him. Consequently we had to handle them with soft gloves, soft words and diplomacy."[26]

The Afro-Caribbean writer Eric Walrond (born in British Guiana, he also spent time in Barbados, Panama, and New York City) wrote in the 1930s that West Indians possessed too much admiration for the English. He, at least, observed a true affection and pride in their British citizenship. It is difficult to judge, in the end, how dearly Afro-Caribbeans held the British Crown in their hearts and minds. But at the very least it is clear that Caribbean workers leveraged their position as British subjects against the Americans when it served their purpose. In his short story "Panama Gold," Walrond explores this theme through a character who returns to Barbados after having lost a leg working on the canal. The man, Mr. Poyer, brags that his status as a British subject forced the canal authorities to pay him damages. Poyer threatened that if he were not paid "I'll sick de British bulldog on all yo' Omericans!" He added, "I let dem understand quick enough dat I wuz a Englishman and not a bleddy American nigger! A' Englishman. . . . And dat dey couldn't do as dey bleddy well please wit' a subject o' de King!"[27]

Recent research on the British West Indies Regiment during World War I also supports the notion that British loyalties were particularly important to the Afro-Caribbeans working on the Panama Canal. They lobbied energetically for the right to participate in the British war effort. As historian Reena Goldthree notes, "Proud of their status as British subjects, islanders enthusiastically supported the Allied cause. During a Flag Day fundraiser in 1915, crowds of 'Loyal Britishers in Bocas del Toro' marched through the city as musicians played 'Rule Britannia.' Female flag sellers—"from tiny girls to elderly women"—sold Union Jack pins, netting hundreds of dollars in

Panamanian silver." It is notable that not only Caribbean immigrants participated in this campaign, but also a great many second-generation Afro-Caribbean Panamanian men and women. In 1915 the British created the British West Indies Regiment and began recruitment throughout the empire—but not yet in Panama. The Panama *Star and Herald* declared that the news "threw the local West Indian colony into a fever of excitement." Committees formed to raise money to send potential recruits to Jamaica to enlist in the war effort. Finally, the lobbying of West Indians in Panama convinced the British to begin recruitment in 1917, and thousands rushed to sign up. Ultimately more than 2,000 of the British West Indies Regiment's 15,600 soldiers came from Panama alone. Recruits would earn good wages and, if injured, disability pensions, and this certainly motivated some given the economic downturn and labor surplus in the Canal Zone at the time. Yet there were also many cases of recruits leaving good jobs to support their king's war effort. As the recruitment offices struggled to keep up with the flood of enlistees, British consul Claude Mallet bragged that "his Majesty's coloured subjects" expressed an "indescribable enthusiasm" for wartime service. The roots of this intense West Indian patriotism toward the British Empire are complex, but a key factor was surely the struggles Caribbeans experienced living under US imperial rule. In that context, they had learned a multitude of times to stress their loyalty to a rival empire as a resource and a strategy.[28]

Afro-Caribbeans remained entangled with the power of both the United States and Britain throughout their time in the Canal Zone and often beyond it as well. Upon completion of the canal construction project, as many towns of the zone were shut down, with forced relocations so the flooding of Gatun Lake could take place, most employees were let go as well. Years of chaos and uncertainly followed, as tens of thousands of workers had to find new jobs in Panama or, in many cases, return to their home islands or settle into new lives in other parts of Central or South America, the Caribbean, or the United States.[29] This complex transition required careful collaboration between American and British officials, who worked alongside United Fruit Company representatives and colonial governments on the home islands to find the best places to send laid-off employees. Afro-Caribbeans thus remained tied to the British Empire, relying on it for help and support long after the canal construction project ended.

Afro-Caribbean workers' identities underwent complex transformations as they adapted to life on the Isthmus of Panama. They felt the scorn of white US bosses and hostility from many Panamanians, but they also felt pride in the tremendous labor they carried out in building the canal. They wrote up their memories in hopes of winning prize money but still found the space to note the racism they had confronted during the construction decade—as well as the physical discomfort and poverty they struggled with in the 1960s. Their worldview became a blend of cultural resources from their home islands and new strategies they developed as they responded to the challenges of life and work on the Isthmus of Panama. Notions of their rights as subjects of the British Empire played a critical role in mediating these diverse influences. If they sometimes felt trapped between the power of the British Empire and the hegemonic US government, they creatively deployed their status as British subjects to gain more ground for maneuvering. The US government's power was far more intertwined with their lives, however, surveilling and tracking them at every step. We turn next to exploring the US personnel records to consider how workers confronted or accommodated themselves to the vast powers of the US empire.

CHAPTER FIVE

The Government's Men

Every archive tells a different story. In the distant suburbs of St. Louis, Missouri, a large building sprawls across seven acres. It holds personnel records for an estimated 100 million civilian and military people employed by the government dating back as far as 1821. This is the National Personnel Records Center (NPRC), a branch of the US National Archives.[1] From soldiers, sailors, and marines in every military engagement since before the Civil War to white collar bureaucrats, from nurses in VA hospitals to the workers who built the Panama Canal—documents on them all are housed there. For the Panama Canal Zone alone there are hundreds of thousands of individuals whose lives have been recorded, tracked, and surveilled.[2]

While the testimonies in Box 25 bring to life the construction decade from the viewpoint of canal workers, the archives at the NPRC disclose a different vision of life and work in the Canal Zone. This was the world from the perspective of the US government—that vast machinery of labor discipline that existed on the Isthmus of Panama for nearly a century. The United States expended vast resources not only to build and maintain the canal but also to maintain documents on its thousands of employees. The records of silver employees had never before been examined by a historian. I wondered, Would I be able to find the men and women in Box 25 at the NPRC—and if I did, would this help me see their lives more fully?

In two visits to the St. Louis archives I examined personnel files for hundreds of Caribbean silver workers. The records gave me a more complete sense of the silver workforce—the islands of origin of the workers, their work lives in the Canal Zone, their family relationships, and their struggles with the US government. The government closely watched all workers, from the lowest messenger boy to carpenters, blacksmiths, teachers, and policemen. I searched for, and found, dozens of men who wrote testimonies for the Isthmian Historical Society competition and then compared their records to the hundreds of other personnel records I examined. When the corporation Family Search digitized many personnel records after I visited the archive, I was able to locate dozens more of the writers in Box 25 as well.

The government records bring workers' experiences to life, not as they remembered them fifty years after first stepping foot on the Isthmus of

Panama but as captured by the government, day to day, in real time. Officials documented every work-related event in an employee's life, from one's hiring to job changes, to gradually increased pay, to ill health, and finally to retirement as an employee reached old age and struggled with impoverishment, worsening health, and finally death. The archive cataloged every accident that befell the workers and every scar or imperfection on their bodies. Typically it provided information about their spouses and children as well.

The meticulous personnel records provide a radically different sense of the workers than the first-person testimonies in Box 25. The government's goal was to catalog and flatten the lives of canal workers to an itinerary of job changes, accidents, disease, and the bodily marks those misfortunes created. Nonetheless it is possible to deploy government records to illuminate the canal workers' lives. What was the measure of a man's life as portrayed in Canal Zone government records? The government's archives provide insight into the complex—and often tense—relationship between Caribbean workers and their government bosses. They suggest both the determination of officials to control their workers and employees' efforts to negotiate concessions from the government at key moments. And they demonstrate the ways the government was at times forced by the spouses of canal workers to intervene in family relations as well.

Every file I accessed at the National Personnel Records Center tracks the individual over many decades. We know that most workers left the job after only a few months or years, particularly during the early, most dangerous years of the construction project. The archives thus make it possible to examine records of only a relatively small subset of the workers, and they tend to be workers who not only began working for the US government during the construction decade but then continued working for another forty or fifty years.[3] This is therefore an exclusive group of workers. The Box 25 writers whose records can be accessed at the NPRC likewise belong to an exceptional group. Their employment records stretch over fifty years or more—these were not transient workers who labored for a year or two and then returned home to Barbados or Antigua. These men and women built homes for themselves on the Isthmus of Panama and, in nearly every case, lived there until their death. They forged a network of kinship ties, they advanced step by step through the occupational hierarchy of the US government, and they confronted the challenges that came with old age, all while living in the Canal Zone or the Republic of Panama. Analyzing the records of the NPRC not only illuminates the experiences of those who built the canal. It introduces us as well to the aftermath of the construction era. In the decades stretching across the mid-twentieth century these men and women created lives and developed community. They experienced the xenophobia and discrimination toward people of African descent that existed in Panama and in the Canal Zone, as well as the very slow march toward equal rights for Afro-Caribbean Panamanians.

As we've seen, the US government attempted to control every aspect of life in the zone, its army of bureaucrats meticulously disciplining the thousands of workers helping to build the canal, assigning them quarters, providing them with meals, overseeing their labor, and, to a significant degree, managing their leisure time. During and after the construction era, officials deployed the silver and gold racial segregation system, vagrancy laws, and the power of deportation to ensure productivity. Yet the personnel records make clear that workers were not powerless but developed ways to carve space for themselves.

Although the canal was formally declared completed in the summer of 1914, dredging work continued for several more years until the seaway could be fully used. In addition, a vast amount of work took place to prepare the zone for the postconstruction era. As Marixa Lasso has shown, the US government decided that effective management of the Canal Zone required eliminating most towns. Officials flooded some towns to create Lake Gatun, but many others they simply annihilated. All these efforts required maintaining a significant workforce—as many as 17,000 silver workers remained on the job by 1920.[4]

In the 1920s the workforce declined significantly as workers completed the construction and transformation of the zone. The US government still required thousands of workers throughout its management of the canal, but layoffs pushed the silver workforce to an all-time low of only 7,600 people. While thousands left the isthmus for jobs across Central America or returned to their home islands, thousands of others settled in the port cities of Panama. The West Indian population in Panama reached 50,000 to 60,000 in the late 1920s.[5] High rates of unemployment, wage cuts, and high rent in Panama's cities combined with growing xenophobia to generate despair in the West Indian community. In the following decades, labor activism and struggles against discrimination in both the zone and the Republic of Panama shaped the lives of Afro-Caribbeans. Meanwhile, thousands of employees worked to maintain the canal, to sustain the houses and offices of the Canal Zone, to run the railroad that ran across the Canal Zone, to feed and wash clothes for employees, and similar tasks. Through all the transformations that they experienced between 1920 and the 1960s, one constant for these workers was the power of the US government in their lives.

We begin with the government's efforts at registering, tracking, and surveilling their workers. From the construction era onward, capturing the essence of their employees (at least as officials saw that essence) on paper required great effort by government officials. A common document—the Application for Photo-Metal Check—involved instructing workers to hold up a number and have their picture taken. Reminiscent of a mug shot, the photos reduced Caribbean laborers to a number. The photographs show the men wearing simple work clothes. The number, their new identifier, is positioned on a stick just beneath their face. Their eyes lock onto the camera with a numb look, clearly pained at being reduced to a few digits. One worker refused to let officials snap his picture, saying it made him feel like a slave. Most men simply suppressed their emotions, their human feelings, and stared sternly ahead of them. Basic information about the workers accompanied the photos: their birthplace, when they arrived on the isthmus, their current job and address. But they also note important information about the men and women—whether they were literate or not, their skin color (black, brown, light black, dark brown, etc.), their height and weight, the color of eyes, and color and kind of hair ("straight, wavy, curly, kinky").

The pages also note "physical deformities or peculiarities, such as scars, moles, and missing members," and thus the pain of working-class life for old and new empires was duly recorded. It is chilling to see these injuries cataloged: upper row of front teeth missing, scar on back of left hand, joint missing third finger right hand, right leg missing, tattooed on both forearms, scar (burn) on right elbow, smallpox in face, scar on jaw, missing first finger right hand, mole under right eye, missing left leg, bent fingers, missing right-hand thumb. On and on the list of deformities continued. Of the hundreds of personnel files I examined, relatively few failed to have some bodily feature identified, for indeed, few Caribbean employees ended their work in the zone without having confronted one or more dangerous accidents.

Officials troubled themselves to record these deformities, not to note painful incidents in employees' lives but to make it easier to track them down. We've noted before that a major strategy enabling workers to assert some control over their lives was their own movement: they constantly changed jobs, residences, and even names, both to improve their working or living conditions but also to elude the watchful eye of government bureaucrats. Therefore, a permanent mark such as a scar or missing finger

THE PANAMA CANAL

MR 63541

APPLICATION FOR PHOTO-METAL CHECK—EMPLOYEES

(Typewrite or write very plainly)

TO EXECUTIVE SECRETARY (through Head of Division)) ----Balboa Hgts.----- C. Z. Sept. 4 191 8

Name............J. Butcher....................... ~~Gold Roll~~ Silver Roll Check No.

Photo-Metal ....

Present ..39471......

Division .....Supply, B. Q. M................... Gang No....105..

Occupation ....Helper...................................., at

..24...cts. per hour

$............per month

Employed, effective..............................., 191..
(For new employers only)

In present rating since................., 191... His service is required
(Date)   (New employees only)

to take the place of........................

on account of .Maintenance..........

Previously employed in The Panama Canal service or by the Panama Railroad Company?........................
(Yes or No)

Citizen of...Gt. Britain...... Date of Birth....5/12/87........ Place of birth......Barbados...
(Give month, day, and year)

Post office address..............Balboa................. Isthmian residence......La Boca......

Arrived on Isthmus.........5/12/05................. Married, ~~single, divorced, or widowed~~
(Cross out those not applicable.)

Color........Black.......... Able to read and write?..Yes......... Able to sign name?....Yes....
(White, black, brown)

Sex Male ~~Female~~ Height........5...ft. ...7...in. Weight........125....lbs.

Physical deformities or peculiarities, such as scars, moles, and missing members?

Missing joint 2nd finger left hand

(FOR GOLD EMPLOYEES ONLY—CIRCLE DESCRIPTION APPLICABLE)

Color of eyes: Blue, chestnut, greenish maroon, maroon, dark maroon, yellow, brown, gray.

Color of hair: Black, blond, chestnut, gray, red, white. BALD ....

Kind of hair: Straight, wavy, curly, kinky............................

Where employed............................ Restricted areas required to enter on

official business ....

Approved and forwarded:

.... O. K. ....
(Head of Division.)   (Foreman.)   (Signature of employee)

(FOR USE OF OFFICIAL PHOTOGRAPHER ONLY)

Photograph taken....DEC 7 19.... Plate No........... 8 / /

Balboa Cristobal Studio

Emergency permit............issued.

Completed and forwarded to Identification Office.......................Initials.........

Recorded and forwarded to applicant............ MAR 31 1919 .....Initials.........

Emergency permit returned and filed........................Initials.........

NOTE.—Two copies of this form must be filled out for each employee. Forms for gold employees required to enter the locks, electric or water supply plants, must be forwarded to the Executive Secretary after approval by head of division. Forms for all other employees will be delivered in person by the employee to the Official Photographer, after approval by head of division. FINGER PRINT IMPRESSIONS WILL BE TAKEN BY OFFICIAL PHOTOGRAPHER.

FIGURE 5.1 John Butcher's application for photo-metal check, National Personnel Records Center

helped bureaucrats struggling to identify who was who. As they marked physical deformities onto their sheet, officials ensured that employees' very bodies would be enlisted in their mission of controlling and tracking them. Officials also noted when there was confusion about a person's name ("also goes by Arnold") or if a person possessed an alias. For example, Leon Pierre Marie Coquelin from Martinique worked as a fireman but was also known by the name Leon Victor; Arnold King went by the name Harold, Cecil Francis sometimes self-identified as Jonathan, and on and on.[6]

The government tracked the occupational and residential history of every employee down to the most precise detail, characterized individuals' overall physical condition, noted the history of accidents and injuries, and specified the native language of each and level of education. Each element reveals more about the workforce. The government's tracking of individuals' occupational histories makes it possible to confirm how frequently employees changed jobs and the degree to which they succeeded in moving into work that paid more or allowed them to work with a kinder foreman. It also makes it possible to examine how and when Caribbeans developed skills and moved from the position of laborer to "artisan" (as US officials termed Black men who worked at skilled occupations). Carpenter or machinist skills, for example, not only resulted in higher salaries but also made workers harder to replace. Since the men and women whose files have been processed by the National Personnel Records Center were typically employees who remained working for the Canal Zone government for many decades, they were also workers who likely possessed some skills.

The personnel records indicate the ways occupations varied by nationality as well as the significance of occupational mobility. In the hundreds of personnel files examined, a few key patterns stand out. Although there were relatively few Latin Americans working in the zone, those who found their way into jobs were much more likely to work from the beginning at skilled positions than were Afro-Caribbeans. Colombians or Costa Ricans were more likely to find jobs as cattlemen or carpenters. Jamaicans were more likely to work in jobs requiring skill and/or literacy than were Caribbeans from other islands (the differences were not as striking as they would surely be if the entire canal construction workforce were considered). Jamaicans only very rarely worked as laborers. Most often they held jobs as clerks or store men, as artisans (coal handlers, for example, or carpenters), or as flagmen or brakemen on the Panama Railroad.[7] Barbadians were more often classified as unskilled laborers, but their workforce was also dominated by jobs involving some skill: messenger, deck employee, tailor, roadmaster, paint and call man, luggerman, or artisan (ironworker, fireman, construction worker). The files confirm that workers changed jobs very often for the first several years they worked on the canal, often switching to a new position as often as within a few months; few held the same job for more than a year or two. Typically, the occupational path would be to change jobs several times over the course of a decade and then land in a better job, one that paid more or required some skill, and then hold it for several decades until old age and various infirmities forced them to apply for disability relief.

Christopher Corbin of Barbados, for example, was born in 1890 and began working as a helper in the Gorgona shops in 1905. He secured a job as brakeman for a while but then moved back down to work as a helper, thus shifting back and forth over the next several years. In 1919 he moved into the better position of ironworker and a year later secured work as a fireman for the Panama Railroad. He remained in that job for more than thirty years.[8]

The writers in Box 25 fit into these patterns. We know from their testimonies that although many began as unskilled laborers, they typically managed to find their way into skilled jobs that paid a better wage. Albert Peters arrived on the isthmus with skills as a carpenter but found himself moving among many different jobs that gradually increased in skill: he graded roads, tended mules, worked as a night watchman, a cooper, a steel cutter, and a diver. Robert Chambers arrived on the isthmus from Ramble, Jamaica, in 1913. The Caribbean hotel waiters were currently engaged in a rare strike, so he found work easily as a strikebreaker. That work, he said in his testimony, didn't agree with him, so he found a job instead as a trackman with a gang. Unfortunately, track work was extremely strenuous. The men would work, he related, from 7:00 A.M. to 4:00 P.M. for ten cents per hour, in sun or rain. "Sometimes we'd be working when a heavy downpour came and we just had to stay there, drenched to the skin, and stay that way until quitting time. Then we board our pump cars to go home. Often we see a train coming so close we barely have time to jump off."

In 1921, as the government decreased the number of workers, Robert Chambers found himself out of a job. Along with four others, he appealed to the roadmaster at Balboa Heights for help. "We the undersigned have taken the presumption of sending you this letter, asking if you could kindly inform us where we could pick up a job. Sir we have been working with Sam Frith on Gang No. 121 Empire, and have worked right through the recent Strike." Now, "anxious for something to do," they wrote desiring work. Correspondence between various government officials demonstrates that efforts were made to determine who had gone on strike and who had not. Once

THE PANAMA CANAL

APPLICATION FOR PHOTO-METAL CHECK—EMPLOYEES

(Typewrite or write very plainly)

To EXECUTIVE SECRETARY (through Head of Division): ......Empire...... C. Z., 8/10, 1918

Name.... Robert Chambers   Gold Roll (New 3 1 7 7 1
                                  Silver Roll Check No.
Division................Supt   Gang No. 1212 Old 97675

Employed, effective........................, as ....Labor.... at { 15 cts. per hour
                         (Date)   (Occupation)   { $...... per month

In present rating since May 1, 1918 His service is required { to take the place of..............
                        (Date)   { on account of..............

Previously employed in The Panama Canal service or by the Panama Railroad Company? ....yes....
                                                                                    (Yes or No)
Citizen of Jamaica   Date of birth dont know   Place of birth...Hamble....
                                     (Give month, day, and year)

Post office address Hamble   Isthmian residence Empire

Arrived on Isthmus Febuary, 1913   Married, single, divorced, widower
                                               (Cross out those not applicable.)

Color Black   Able to read and write? yes   Able to sign name? yes
       (White, black, brown)   (CIRCLE DESCRIPTION APPLICABLE)

Sex Male   Height .... ft. .... in. Weight .... lbs.
    Female

Physical deformities or peculiarities, such as scars, moles, and missing members?

....

FOR GOLD EMPLOYEES ONLY
Color of eyes: Blue, chestnut, greenish maroon, maroon, dark maroon, yellow.
Color of hair: Black, blond, chestnut, gray, red, white. BALD.
Kind of hair: Straight, wavy, curly, kinky.

Where employed .... Restricted areas required to enter on

official business ....

Approved and forwarded: R. D. Cannon
    Acting Head of Division   (Signature of person employing)

FOR USE OF OFFICIAL PHOTOGRAPHER ONLY
                                  Plate No. 1225   Balboa Studio
Photograph taken DEC 30 1918   Cristobal
Emergency permit issued.
Completed and forwarded to Identification Office   Initials........
Recorded and forwarded to applicant APR 14 1919 Initials........
Emergency permit returned and filed.   Initials........

NOTE.—Two copies of this form must be filled out for each employee. Forms for gold employees required to enter the locks, electric or extra supply plants, must be forwarded to the Executive Secretary after approval by head of division. Forms for all other employees will be delivered in person by the employee to the Official Photographer, after approval by head of division. FINGER PRINT IMPRESSIONS WILL BE TAKEN BY OFFICIAL PHOTOGRAPHER.

FIGURE 5.2 Robert Chambers's application for photo-metal check,
National Personnel Records Center

officials verified that Chambers and the other men had continued working during the strike, they found them jobs. This enabled Chambers to become a rare man who kept working for the Canal Zone government after completion of the project. He continued as laborer for a few more years until, in 1924, he learned of a better job available as a porter. He began that job in 1924 and stayed until 1952, when the government classified him as "unfit for service due to physical disability resulting from advanced age."

Although he clearly had benefited, more than once, from his decision to help break strikes conducted by his fellow workers, Chambers also knew how to fight for better pay or working conditions. According to his personnel file he repeatedly pushed the government for increased pay, in 1926, 1927, 1929, and 1931, making the case each time that his work was good and that he had a family to support. Most times he received a pay raise. In 1938 he requested to be upgraded from porter to office helper. An internal memo demonstrates that the color line was still alive and well in the Canal Zone's labor management strategies. Officials reflected that they would prefer to keep Chambers categorized as a porter because office helper positions were typically reserved for US citizens—yet they did want to raise Chambers's pay. The government's quandary was heightened by the fact that Chambers's job included cleaning toilets, which US citizens would not want to do. The government in this case decided to raise his pay due to his fine service but keep him categorized as a porter. In 1940, without any debate indicating how or why conditions changed, the government finally upgraded him to office helper and again raised his pay.[9]

Harrigan Austin's case helps us understand the struggle many workers faced in trying to develop an income that could support a large family. Born in 1887 in Barbados, he arrived in Panama in 1905 after thirteen days at sea. Unlike most workers, he arrived with the experience and tools of a carpenter. He landed a job repairing quarters with a foreman, he said, who knew nothing about carpentry. Although his work life was likely easier than most workers given his skill level, he nonetheless found it difficult. He felt, he said, like a slave. There were no women to do the laundry, he related, and men bathed and washed their clothes in the same river used by horses and cattle. After several years working as a carpenter, Austin switched to a new job as a driller. By 1913, when the zone was being forcibly depopulated, Harrigan had a wife and four children. They lived in a home he had built himself on a hillside near the railroad but had been ordered to leave. "On account of the present depopulation of the zone I have been noticed to remove same by the end of this month. . . . on account of my present condition with such family expenses having a family of six to support and my wife has just had her last baby I had to spend all the dimes I had for midwife and Doctor so that I have failed to provide such things as are necessary for removing." Thus he requested an additional month before he would be required to leave. The file provides no information on the government's response.

Perhaps due to insufficient wages, Austin decided soon after this to make ends meet by farming. He worked at this for nearly sixteen years. Meanwhile his family grew. By 1931 he and his wife cared for nine children. That year he returned to work as a carpenter and continued working until terminated in 1953. In 1954, as part of his application for disability relief payments, Austin sent a handwritten note describing his career:

Began work Oct. 10 Lisle Austin Bas Obispo, carpenter, foreman
    Mr. Briggs
Worked about two months
Removed to Paraiso under name as John Springer
About Dec. 1905 Carpenter until Oct. 1906 Took malaria
Worked again Feb. 1907 Lisle Austin Mr. Briggs general foreman
    building construction
Transferred to Caimita as Albert Austin latter part of 1907 transferred
    from building construction to car repair and house repairs by same
    name Albert Austin
General foreman was Mr. Dickey until 1908 about July ended by
    reduction of force
Then worked at Pedro Miguel as Harrigan Austin from about
    August 1908 to 1909 carpenter for quartermaster.

The note continued relating Austin's entire career; this excerpt captures his constant occupational mobility and name changing as well as the struggles with disease that characterized the work lives of most Caribbeans.

In addition to pushing for better pay, Austin relied on the government for help with family matters. Like so many men and women of Caribbean descent, some in the Austin family saw Panama as just one stop in a larger pattern of migration. When an older son or daughter took off to return home or to migrate onward to Cuba or the United States, it could become difficult to keep in touch. Thus, in 1935 Austin wrote government officials for help finding his daughter Lillian Alberta Austin. She had left for New York City thirteen years earlier, and he lost contact with her. Lillian was born in the Canal Zone, at Pedro Miguel, in 1910. Austin had addresses for her in Brooklyn or Manhattan up until 1934; he also provided an address for his brother

William Austin in New York City. Austin seems not to have received a response to this query, so three years later he wrote again. "I have lost sight of my daughter in N.Y. USA for the last four years and has failed in all efforts to find her. She is a very dutiful child, her mother is dead, and I would be glad to get any possible help to find, tis expected that some misfortion has befallen her, and she is supposed to be in confinement in some institution whether hospital asylum or reformatory." Government officials were puzzled by Austin's request since his personnel file had never included a daughter named Lillian, and he had not personally tried to contact his brother in New York for information. Nonetheless, they forwarded his request on to the New York Police Department. Police investigated and visited the daughter's last known address. They wrote that they could find no information about her, and records showed she had never been arrested.[10]

Like Harrigan Austin, other workers whose testimonies sit in Box 25 appear in the personnel files, their careers tracked by officials for many years. A lengthy file, for example, followed the career of Constantine Parkinson, who had lost his leg in the railroad accident of July 1913, over the next several decades. His file begins with reports by witnesses to that accident. One witness, C. C. Snediker, saw him attempt to board a fast-moving ledgerwood train. "He either misjudged the speed of the train or slipped, and fell the last car passed over his right leg below the knee, cutting if off and crushing his left foot." As Parkinson wrote in his testimony, after his surgery he was finally discharged in November 1913. For one year he received disability compensation from the government; in 1914 he returned to the hospital and was fitted with an artificial leg. He had been promised that a job would be waiting for him after the one year, but when he reported to the construction and engineering department, officials said they had nothing for him. So, he appealed to chief engineer George Goethals: "I therefore bring the matter to your notice, with the fullest confidence that you will do the best you can for me. I am a Panamanian, 20 years old, having a grandmother 64 years old of which I am the sole support also a Mother. I am quite willing to work, not dictating to you sir but if I could get a position as stationary switch tender or watchman I am quite capable of handling the job." It took time for officials to find Parkinson a job, but with a supervisor's praise in mind ("I find him to be a very worthy and hard working boy") they hired him in 1915 as a telephone attendant. In following years, he took jobs in succession as switch tender, as helper in charge of issuing tools, and finally by 1917 he secured work as a watchman in the receiving and forwarding agency. He continued working in the latter job until his retirement in 1957.

THE PANAMA CANAL

APPLICATION FOR PHOTO-METAL CHECK—EMPLOYEES
(Typewrite or write very plainly)

MR 63165

To EXECUTIVE SECRETARY (through Head of Division):

Cristobal. C. Z., Dec. 20th 191-8

Name Constantine Parkinson. Gold Roll Check No. { Photo-Metal 50129
Silver Roll
{ Present 115734

Division, RECEIVING AND FORWARDING AGENCY. Gang No. Reg. No. 1728

Occupation Watchman , at { .... cts. per hour
{ $ 1.10 per month day

Employed, effective , 191
(For new employees only)

In present rating since June 1917, 191. His service is required { to take the place of
(Date) (New employees only) { on account of

Previously employed in The Panama Canal service or by the Panama Railroad Company? Yes
(Yes or No)

Citizen of Panama Date of birth 12th Nov. 1884 Place of birth Colon.
(Give month, day, and year)

Post office address Cristobal. C. Z. Isthmian residence Colon.

Arrived on Isthmus Married, single, divorced, or widowed
(Cross out those not applicable)

Color Black. Able to read and write? Yes Able to sign name?
(White, black, brown)

Sex Male Height 5 ft. 8 ½ in. Weight 112 lbs.
Female

Physical deformities or peculiarities, such as scars, moles, and missing members?

lost right leg.

(FOR GOLD EMPLOYEES ONLY—CIRCLE DESCRIPTION APPLICABLE)
Color of eyes: Blue, chestnut, greenish maroon, maroon, dark maroon, yellow, brown, gray.
Color of hair: Black, blond, chestnut, gray, red, white. BALD
Kind of hair: Straight, wavy, curly, kinky.

Where employed Cristobal. Dock. Restricted areas required to enter on

official business

Approved and forwarded:

(signature) o. _(signature)_ Constantine Parkinson
(Head of Division.) (Foreman.) (Signature of employee.)

(FOR USE OF OFFICIAL PHOTOGRAPHER ONLY)

Photographed JAN 16 1919 Plate No. Balboa Cristobal Studio
Emergency permit issued.
Completed and forwarded to Identification Office. Initials
Recorded and forwarded to applicant Initials
Emergency permit returned and filed Initials

NOTE.—Two copies of this form must be filled out for each employee. Forms for gold employees required to enter the locks, electric or water power plants, must be forwarded to the Executive Secretary after approval by head of division. Forms for all other employees will be delivered in person by the employee to the Official Photographer, after approval by head of division. FINGER PRINT IMPRESSIONS WILL BE TAKEN BY OFFICIAL PHOTOGRAPHER.

FIGURE 5.3 Constantine Parkinson's application for photo-metal check, National Personnel Records Center

During his long career working for the Canal Zone government, Parkinson repeatedly fought for his right to a new artificial leg. In 1919 he reminded officials they had said he would be entitled to a new leg after seven years, or sooner if the artificial limb did not last. He declared that it was nearly impossible to use his leg and appealed for a new one. Officials debated among themselves at some length whether Parkinson should be required to pay the cost of the new artificial leg but in the end decided to provide it to him at no expense. Parkinson appealed again in 1925, 1929, and 1938, and each time he received a new artificial limb from the government. In 1946 he felt compelled to order a new part for his leg or face immobility. He did so and asked for reimbursement for thirty dollars, but this time the government refused, saying it needed to be cleared through the appropriate office in advance.

In these ways the years rolled by for Constantine Parkinson. In 1956 government officials began preparing for his termination. A physical exam suggested that he had hypertension and could no longer do his job effectively. But he was now a union man, a member of the American Federation of State, County and Municipal Employees, and the union representative involved himself in the case. He pointed out that Parkinson's diagnosis of hypertension was caused by his not wearing his glasses to correct for faulty near vision during the exam. The examining doctor had failed to inquire whether he normally wore glasses. A further physical exam showed that the glasses eliminated the hypertension problem, and Parkinson was allowed to remain on the job. A year later, as the pier where Parkinson worked was to be shut down, he again faced termination. His union representative intervened another time, arguing that his good work as union steward and chairman of the recreation committee should win him special dispensation as a reward. The union noted that Parkinson remained in good health and was doing good work. However, officials determined that union work was not a sufficient reason for Parkinson to be given special treatment. Parkinson completed his last day of work after forty-eight years on November 30, 1957.[11]

The case of Samuel Smith shows how deeply government officials became involved in personal family relationships. Smith was born in Jamaica in 1894 and began working on the canal project in 1912. Like other employees he changed jobs often the first few years. His first job was as a laborer helping to build the enormous lock gates. Over the next years he shifted to various departments, always as laborer, before landing in the dredging division in 1915. He would remain in that department the rest of his career, working initially as laborer and then moving up to the semiskilled position of oiler. He worked for the government for forty-four years; at its highest his wage climbed to \$52.50 per month, or just \$1.75 each day. It was difficult to raise a family on this low wage, and many workers, like Smith, ran into difficulties. The most acute problems often occurred in the 1930s, when Panama shared in the global economic crisis.

The US government in the Canal Zone accepted its responsibility to help ensure that families were united. If an employee could demonstrate that a child or spouse was back home in Jamaica or Barbados, officials would provide documentation allowing family members to come to Panama and reunite with their parents or partner. But just as officials had trouble tracking and surveilling their employees due to their regular changes in jobs or residences and adopting new names, so they found it challenging to keep family relationships straight. The personnel files include many cases similar to Samuel Smith's. Smith had successfully applied for a certificate of identity to bring his wife from Jamaica to Panama in 1925. In 1930 he applied for a similar certificate in order to bring a seventeen-year-old daughter, Clarissa, from Jamaica. Yet, officials noted that in 1929 he had stated that he was a single man and had no dependents. In 1931 officials attempted to clear up the confusion. In an interview Smith explained that his child Clarissa had been living in Jamaica with a grandmother who had recently died. She had no other family members in Jamaica, and so, although he had been sending her money, he now needed to bring her to Panama. Officials puzzled over whether Smith could indeed have fathered a child in Jamaica before moving to the isthmus, when he would have been only sixteen years of age. In the end, though, they chalked all this up to different cultural patterns among West Indians. After interviewing Smith, C. A. McIlvaine wrote, "It is my conjecture that due to my lack of familiarity with the West Indian dialect I understood Smith's statement that he was 'single' as indicating that his civil status was that of a man who had never married. More experience, has of course, taught me that such a statement may merely mean that the subject is separated temporarily or permanently from his spouse." They granted the necessary documentation for Clarissa to join her father.[12]

Bigger problems awaited Smith, however, and his story in this case demonstrates how marital conflicts generated challenges for government officials as well. Joan Flores-Villalobos has shown that US officials disapproved of West Indian cohabitation and associated women in particular with sexual vice and prostitution. Yet ultimately, they often turned a blind eye, she has found, as long as the relationships didn't harm labor productivity.[13] The personnel files however demonstrate that often the US government felt compelled to become involved in West Indian relationships, particularly when marriages or common-law partnerships broke up. In such situations the male canal employees were expected to provide for any children. When they did not, their former spouses or common-law partners often went to the government to complain and ask the government to force payment. Marital relations between Afro-Caribbeans were in many cases not permanent. Caribbean women often had traveled to the isthmus to be with menfolk who were working for the Canal Zone government. According to the 1912 census of the Canal Zone, there were 6,175 Afro-Caribbean women there. The census listed only approximately half of these women as working for a wage — most often as domestic servants or laundresses. However, the census only counted as working those who worked for the Isthmian Canal Commission or for private families in the zone. Many other women undoubtedly worked in the port cities of the Republic of Panama or took episodic work such as sewing or washing into their homes. Thus, it is important not to put too much credence in these statistics. Nonetheless, the numbers suggest that many Caribbean women depended partially or entirely on their male partners to make ends meet. When marriages ended in divorce, or when common-law marriages fell apart, and particularly if there were children involved, the women would face severe economic vulnerability. Men were responsible for supporting their children after a marital partnership ended; when they did not, the personnel records make very clear, women found ways to assert their rights particularly by nudging the government to help them. Cases like the following one shed light not only on the failed marital partnerships among Caribbeans but also the economic struggles distraught women faced and their assertive efforts to force the government to assist them.

In June 1933 Edith Blake wrote Paul Wilson, a US government official, to complain that Samuel A. Smith "refused from maintaining his child" who had been born in February of that year. He had given three dollars for her support in March and again in May, but nothing since. Smith complained he could not easily provide help for Edith Blake and her child on his low wages but confirmed that he would give her five dollars of his commissary book each month. Yet Edith Blake soon had to request help again. Her complaints stretched into the next year and the next until a decade of negotiations and complaints revealed themselves. In December 1931 Edith Blake wrote directly to Samuel Smith: "I would like to know what the resing why you did not send the five dollar in the month of November you have only send three. Please send and tell why you don't send the amount can a child feed by three dollars for a hold month please send me a reply." Smith replied that he had been taken ill and hospitalized and owed three dollars for the hospital bill so had gotten behind on payments. He would do better in the future, he said. Six months later Smith informed the government that as he had two new children to support, younger than Edith Blake's child, and that because the government had cut his wages, he decided to give Blake only $2.50 per month. The government ordered him to give Blake four dollars monthly instead. In months to come Smith repeatedly noted that his and his children's illnesses made it impossible to pay. Officials expressed their exhaustion over Smith's claims that illness kept him from making the payments and continued ordering him to pay.[14]

In 1934 Edith Blake wrote again. Smith had told her he would not support her child much longer, she claimed. "He has a woman in Colón working obiah for him not to support his child, so he can't be fired from his job. He also said I can write you as often as I like, it won't make no difference to him, for in the long run it will be the same as before." It is striking to see this reference to Obeah, the syncretic religious practice that blends African and Christian influences. Obeah was outlawed in Jamaica in 1760 to protect slavery from potential rebellions fueled by the practice.[15] Smith's response ignored the issue of Obeah but focused instead on the economic distress his family faced. "I am legally married now and have three children by my present wife, ages 2 years, 1 year, and 9 months. I owe the landlord three months rent, a total of $24.00 and he has threatened to put me out if I do not pay at once; so I will have to borrow money in order to keep my home." Edith Blake, on the other hand, he noted, had only one child by him and was now living with another man. He knew he must make payments to her or lose his job, but as he earned only $47.50 per month, he found it impossible. Edith Blake's appeals kept arriving. "My dear Gentleman, with tears in mine eyes I sit again to address you this letter. . . . Help me along with my poor child, for its very hard, some mornings he hasn't no tea to drink and has a father working every day and would not support him."

Some officials were beginning to waver in their commitment to make Smith pay. Smith's supervisor, P. A. White, wrote his superiors to suggest that Smith be relieved of his obligation. He characterized Smith as a good worker. "I have known him personally for several years and, in my opinion, this woman is imposing on him. He claims that she is now living with another man, requires no additional support, and is only asking for it in order to make trouble for him. Smith says she told him some time ago that she is going to make him lose his job."[16]

White's attempt to advocate on Smith's behalf failed. His superior was firm in response. "This man Smith has been procrastinating for several years. He has several times been threatened with suspension and discharge but always manages to find another excuse. . . . Although Smith claims he cannot afford to support his child, we must insist. The excuse that the woman is 'trying to get his job' is put forth by most of these people. The women always tell another story and since we cannot judge between them we have insisted that the father support the children . . . until they become self-supporting." Finally, "the fact that he has a family beyond his income is no fault of the Panama Canal, he should have thought of that before he established the family." This official renewed the command that Smith pay four dollars per month and stated he would be suspended if he failed to comply.[17]

Over the years the letters of complaint and Smith's responses continued and officials expressed weariness. In August 1938, Smith provided details on the financial pressures he faced. He now had four children and a wife to support, expenses for transportation to and from work (he lived in Ancon), an aged mother in Jamaica who needed his financial help, and only fifty dollars per month to cover the expenses. In addition, he introduced a new issue for the officials' consideration: "Regarding the paternity of Edith Blake's child I have always been in doubt. This phase of the matter I have always held back in answering her complaints, but it now seems in fairness to myself I should bring to the front." He never lived with Edith Blake, he said, although he admitted to "relations that lend plausibility to her claim that I am the father of her child." On the basis of that unproven claim, he had supported the child for many years. He noted he had never been allowed to see the child's birth certificate and again noted that he doubted very much he was the father. Despite Smith's robust effort to relinquish his financial responsibility, government officials remained unyielding. A handwritten note by one declared that "this man is a chronic offender — his file is a mess of complaints and ignored promises — he should have been fired before this." Officials did order that he be allowed to see the birth certificate, but they also ordered Smith suspended for five days.[18]

Since the letters of complaint and Smith's retorts continued for so many years, we can mark the events in the life of the Smith family by tracing his reasons for nonpayment. His wife or children fell ill and spent time in the hospital; he faced a wage cut; and in 1940, his mother in Jamaica died and he incurred extra expenses. We also see the expenses Edith Blake confronted — needing to pay dues for her child's school or providing basics like food and clothing. Government threats of suspension or discharge continued to be issued, Smith promised to make up his payments, and then after a few more months there would be another long letter of complaints from Edith Blake. In some she accused Smith of lying when he said he had talked things over with her. In another case the government realized, after she complained about nonpayment, that she had in fact cashed the checks. They accused her of taking advantage of the situation, "even to the point of distortion of facts."[19]

Finally the Smith and Blake case ends. Smith worked for the government for fifteen more years. He was terminated and provided with disability relief in March 1956, at the age of sixty-two. He had worked for the US government for thirty-four years. He had one son in the US Army who sent the family fifty dollars each month. Smith stated that he had no savings or investments.[20] The government awarded him disability pay of forty-five dollars per month to help provide for a family of five children and a wife. In his brief testimony for the Isthmian Historical Society competition, Smith looked back upon his years of labor. "My greatest experience was the construction of the Panama Canal, and I am more than proud to be among the many old timers who have helped so willingly in giving a hand in building this masterpiece. I am even more proud to be alive today, thank God, to enjoy the beautiful scenery and to witness its important participation in commerce to the world."[21]

The case of Samuel Smith and Edith Blake was unusual in stretching on for more than a decade. But in other ways it reflected a common pattern in which Caribbean women fought for their right to child support, as they saw it, by involving canal officials in their cases. The negotiations also provide insight into Caribbean men's and women's struggles to make ends meet on the relatively low wages paid to canal workers. The case of Clement Boyce and his wife Emma provided remarkable detail about family finances as they negotiated over his child support payments. Clement Boyce was a carpenter who had arrived on the isthmus from Barbados in 1909 at the age of twenty-one. He and his wife Emma had four children and shared a home for many years. In 1938, however, Emma Boyce wrote the executive secretary of the Canal Zone government to complain that Clement was not giving her sufficient support. "Sir I want to ask you if you think that a five dollars ($5.00) in Commissary Book and five dollars ($5.00) in cash can support myself and three children in the home." Clement Boyce responded to the executive secretary by laying out his financial commitments. As a carpenter he received fifty-five to sixty-two dollars in wages each month. He had $7.50 deducted for his rent each month and in addition had to pay someone to cook and clean for him and wash his clothes. He insisted that he was giving his wife five dollars from his commissary, not just once a month but every time it was issued. He further argued that most of his children were now old enough to be working and bringing some money into the household. Seymour Paul, the personnel director, informed Emma Boyce that if she was unhappy with the amount of money Boyce was providing, she would need to take the issue to the courts. But he also instructed Boyce to make regular payments and provide evidence of having done so.[22]

Working-class Caribbean women on the Isthmus of Panama navigated a difficult journey between desires for respectability and white assumptions that they engaged in sexual vice. While officials tolerated cohabitation and tried to remain uninvolved in West Indians' personal relationships unless conflicts threatened labor productivity, the personnel records also demonstrate that officials felt a responsibility to ensure male workers continued providing support for their families after marriage or partnership disintegrated. Further they show that women pushed government officials as a way to receive the support they were due. Appeals to government officials became an important resource for vulnerable and financially challenged West Indian women. Yet their success at resolving problems was mixed at best, and their affairs were certainly judged through the gaze of white male government officials.[23]

US government officials created an archive that reflected their goals of managing and disciplining their large, diverse, and often cantankerous workforce. The vast government bureaucracy embedded officials' power into the most minute factual details they collected and recorded about thousands of workers across the isthmus. They provide a treasure trove of information about workers' lives. Much as the government archives sought to flatten workers' experiences and deploy their recordkeeping to better control the workforce, the trials and tribulations of Caribbean men and women leap to three-dimensional life in these pages. Capturing workers' personal lives, their physical struggles, and even their intimate relationships, the records also display workers' resistance to the powerful bureaucracy. They document working men and women fighting for better pay or working conditions, seeking help to find lost family members, demanding assistance with a disability, or deploying the government's power to win child support payments from estranged partners. Ironically the government archives sometimes reveal more about West Indian men and women than do the workers' own testimonies in Box 25. This contradiction reminds us that the Box 25 testimonies were clouded by the limitations of individual experience, including the deprivations of old age and poverty. Despite the intentions of government officials, their imperial archive documents the avenues by which working men and women deployed strategies for building lives of value in Panama.

CHAPTER SIX

The Long Life of the Archive

In 1963 Jules LeCurrieux ended his essay for the Isthmian Historical Society competition by stressing the crucial role played by the true pioneers, the West Indian workers. "Now we have lived to see the old Ditch dug." He noted their suffering and sacrifices, and the thousands who had died. "Who dug the Canal? Who suffered most, *even until now*? Who died most? Who but the West Indian negroes." Furthermore, he said Afro-Caribbean workers had never received the compensation nor even the "worthy praise" they deserved.[1] LeCurrieux's powerful demand for recognition, and his blend of pride and bitterness, have had a long life. Even today, many Afro-Caribbeans in Panama and across the diaspora feel that their community's significant role has been neglected or erased altogether.

Did the Caribbean workers who entered the Isthmian Historical Society competition succeed in making their voices heard, or did colonial power relations and the exploitation workers faced continue to haunt the reception and deployment of the testimonies? As Michel-Rolph Trouillot reminded us, power shapes not only the collection of evidence and the creation of the archive, but also the ways scholars choose to retrieve certain facts in order to develop their narratives. The creation of a narrative about the past is not only an opportunity to highlight a hidden history, but also a critical moment in which silences produced by existing power relations shape the process of historical production.[2] We might add that these processes can be shaped as well by community-generated projects to document and highlight a neglected history. This chapter examines how the history of West Indian workers on the canal has been remembered by historians as well as the efforts being made by archivists and community activists to shape historical memory and understanding.

There are many accounts of the construction project written in the early twentieth century that include observations of the West Indian workforce. They provide a baseline of white perceptions of West Indian workers. Travelers like Winifred James or the census taker and zone policeman Harry Franck viewed Caribbean workers from the outside, with a sort of racist condescension. Like canal commission officials we explored in earlier chapters, these observers stressed the laziness and lack of productivity of

West Indians. Willis Abbot, in his popular book on the canal project published in 1913, struck a common tone: "The Jamaica negro is a natural loafer. Of course he works when he must, but betwixt the mild climate, the kindly fruits of the earth and the industry of his wife or wives, that dire necessity is seldom forced upon him." They were good-natured, grinning, and childlike in the eyes of Abbot—yet occasionally Caribbean workers were also prone to trouble. He noted accurately that riots occasionally broke out on ships headed for Panama. The latter fact caused some cognitive dissonance for Abbot, and he didn't attempt to resolve the seeming contradiction between these diverse observations.[3]

Likewise, the writer Farnham Bishop observed that Caribbean workers were "peaceable and law-abiding fellows, but exceedingly lazy, and unbelievably stupid."[4] Often such descriptions would then be accompanied by the comment that the Caribbeans refused to work more than they wanted, thereby forcing officials to create a workforce nearly twice as large as needed on any given day. That such strategic deployment of their labor signified intelligence and resistance among Caribbean workers seemed beyond the comprehension of white observers.[5]

Winifred James, the well-to-do Australian novelist and travel writer, acknowledged her own parochialism as she began a tour of the Caribbean. Arriving in Jamaica she felt unsettled, she commented, because she had never been among so many "black, brown, and yellow" faces. Rather than calling Caribbeans lazy, she simply noted that the "Jamaican negro . . . won't work if he doesn't want to." Yet like others, James's perspective on Caribbean workers included a dose of racism. She saw them as lying whenever necessary and "among themselves they chatter ceaselessly like children." She also found them to be insensitive and apathetic "in the presence of pain." James described a man "whose foot had been cut off by a passing train [and] was left lying on the line till a white man came by and found him. The negroes had gone up to him, looked at him, and passed on, apparently quite indifferent."[6] Throughout her book, James mixed condescension with a degree of empathy for the plight of West Indians. She referred to them as savage yet noted the injustices they faced. "One's sympathy goes assuredly to the negro. He has never seen justice, he has never . . . had justice. The white man took him out of his own land whether he liked it or not. He dragged him away to a white man's world; he beat him, robbed him of his freedom, stole the reward of his labour and violated his women. That was the negro's first knowledge of civilization."[7]

James was also struck by the contrast between West Indians and African Americans. Jamaicans and Barbadians dominated the labor force, she reported, because officials found African Americans to be "insolent and difficult to manage." The Caribbeans "had to be coaxed and jollied along, [they] . . . understood authority." She seemed taken aback by the level of knowledge West Indians had received as a result of British colonial education, but as with so many things she managed to turn it into a patronizing and racialized joke. Jamaican "negroes," she stressed, loved words of four syllables or more. "Long words are to them what beer is to the working classes in England. They don't drink excessively, but they must have their intoxication somehow. Long words, no matter what the meaning is, fill them with the spirit of their own greatness and warm them with the wine of their seeming wisdom."[8]

It also struck many white travelers that West Indians, for all their merits or faults, had to be treated carefully. Joseph Bucklin Bishop, secretary of the Isthmian Canal Commission during the construction era, noted that the Caribbeans dominating the workforce were profoundly aware of their status as subjects of the British Empire — or "as they always style themselves, British 'objects.'" Constantly issues emerged that had to be negotiated between the British consul Claude Mallet and the Isthmian Canal Commission, he noted. In his condescending way, Bishop conceded that foremen had to take care in their treatment of the West Indian workers. "They were very 'cocky' about being rebuked or hurried, and if a foreman spoke to them harshly would draw themselves up with amusing dignity and say: 'You can't address me in that manner, sah! I am a British object!'"[9]

Labor recruiter William Karner noted similarly the complexity of overseeing Caribbean workers because they demanded to be treated with respect. While he described Caribbeans as childlike, he clearly found them challenging, and he and his foremen were forced to adapt. When Karner hired a track foreman from the United States, the man quickly found it too difficult to work with Caribbeans and decided to catch the next steamer home. He explained his decision: "The foremen of the gangs over there do not give orders, they make requests. For instance, if a foreman wants some railroad ties moved, he says, 'Mr. Jones, will you and Mr. Smith please place that sleeper over here.'" The track foreman complained, "With a good track gang of Mississippi negroes I can do more work in a day than those British objects will do in a week, and I think I will go back where I can earn my money." Karner convinced the man to remain and try again. The foreman went back

to work and instructed his foreman (himself West Indian) to stop address-
ing workers as "Mr." The latter reluctantly agreed but insisted on referring
to workers instead as "gentlemen." Apparently giving up, the US track boss
soon returned home to the United States. If we read past the humor and racism of this anecdote, we're left with a situation in which Caribbean workers
insisted on kind and respectful treatment from their bosses.[10]

The census taker and policeman Harry Franck explained that Caribbeans
were an unusually educated group. He compared the West Indians to the
Spaniards working on the canal, who were almost all, he believed, illiterate.
In contrast, Franck noted, the "negroes from the British West Indies, thanks
to their good fortune in being ruled over by the world's best colonist, could
almost invariably read and write; many of those shoveling in the 'cut' have
been trained in trigonometry." In short, when reading traveler accounts of
the construction project, even as one tires of the racialized references to West
Indian inferiority, gradually an unintended meaning emerges of a Caribbean
workforce able to shape their relationship to white bosses.

In these contemporary accounts, filled with conflicting and contradictory statements, we see how racism combined with a grudging acceptance
of West Indian strengths to shape the observations of officials and travelers.
Moving forward a few decades, we encounter a very different group analyzing and interpreting the actions of Caribbean workers: the historians. The
first notable history of the canal's construction was written by Gerstle Mack
in 1944. An impressive work, *The Land Divided* sweeps from the early days of
Spanish exploration on the isthmus to the completion of the canal in 1914.
Mack had been trained as an architect and served in two world wars, including eighteen months in London working with the Office of Strategic
Services. *The Land Divided* is eloquently written in an engaging and accessible way. It tells a top-down story focused on diplomacy and engineering. In
the nearly 200 pages on the US construction project, there is little information about workers—virtually no mention of them until a penultimate
chapter—and there the discussion relies heavily on officials' views of the
workforce. Labor is a problem to be managed and controlled. Workers must
be disciplined. Mack acknowledged the racial segregation system that pervaded the zone but seemed defensive of official policies. "During the construction period as well as later instances of actual brutality appear to have
been exceedingly rare." Ultimately, Mack summarized, "relations between
the laborers and the canal administration were on the whole satisfactory after
the first year."[11]

Gerstle Mack's book seems to have served as a model for David McCullough's best-selling tale, *The Path Between the Seas*, published in 1977. This book by the enormously popular McCullough was the first major work published after the testimonies in Box 25 became available.[12] The books by Mack and McCullough read quite similarly, even to the use of common phrases, and although McCullough's book begins later, with the French effort, its narrative arc is remarkably similar to that created by Mack. Both books lavish attention on the technocratic side of the project—the engineering, technology, and medical breakthroughs. Yet there are differences. McCullough, presenting a heroic tale at a time when the United States was staggering from its failure in Vietnam, gave to his history a more emphatic tone of US triumphalism. The great men who led the effort were not flawless in his telling, yet they were intrepid, undaunted—nearly Herculean. McCullough also wrote at a time when history as a discipline had been transformed as new social and cultural methodologies spread, and simultaneously the civil rights movement had changed white people's understanding of race and race relations. So, McCullough handled issues of race with more awareness and sensitivity than did Gerstle Mack. Add to this McCullough's engaging and humane writing style, and you have an author who, even as he added a tone of boosterism and focused most of his attention on the great men who led the effort, still managed to write warmly about the humblest Caribbean diggers and track shifters.

McCullough in *The Path Between the Seas* was also more cognizant of racial discrimination, and more frankly critical of it. The major consideration of Caribbean laborers comes in a chapter titled "Life and Times," which is concerned as well with the experiences of white US citizens, European workers, and Panamanians. This chapter is the closest the book comes to providing a social historical approach to life and work during the US construction era. The section on Black Caribbean workers constitutes about ten pages of the thirty-five-page chapter.

McCullough begins his discussion of West Indian labor by noting that "to judge by many published accounts, the whole enormous black underside of the caste system simply did not exist." He then brings to life the challenges they faced, noting with empathy that "they too were making a new life in an alien land. . . . They too were raising families, experiencing homesickness, fear, illness, or exhilaration in the success of the work." He notes, accurately, that the gold and silver segregation system shaped every aspect of workers' lives. "It was as clearly drawn . . . as anywhere in the Deep South or the most rigid colonial enclave in Africa." McCullough provided several paragraphs on the specific form discrimination took in housing, food, health care, wages, and entertainment. Yet then he carefully backed away from acknowledging the brutality of the racial segregation system. One might assume, he said, "that this was all the most blatant kind of racial injustice. And in a very large measure, of course, it was, but not entirely." He ascribed racial discrimination to the dynamics of supply and demand: doctors were in short supply, and "common laborers" from impoverished Caribbean islands were abundantly available "and expected no better than what they got." Furthermore, they were foreigners and so had no leverage in Washington, DC. Finally, he concluded, it was "unquestionably true" that "no labor army in history had ever been so well paid, well fed, well cared for." Since McCullough had just established, in discussing racial discrimination, that the *white* labor army in the Canal Zone was in fact far better paid, fed, and cared for, this was an odd claim.[13]

McCullough made extensive use of the testimonies in Box 25 to bring individual workers' experiences to life. Their vibrant language combines with McCullough's writing skill to make for stirring stories of life and work in the Canal Zone. The excerpts chosen by McCullough provide glimpses of occasional racism, the difficulties of the work, and the mobility of Caribbean workers. The tone McCullough ascribes to the Box 25 writers is overall one of tremendous respect for Goethals and the project, even amid the discrimination and difficult conditions. McCullough highlights one man, for example, who praised Goethals as "calm, principled, dignified."[14]

Throughout the book, the passages encourage readers to care about Black Caribbean workers, and they enable readers to imagine a bit of their lives. Yet the world his text conjures up is remarkably close to the official narrative about the canal. Much like John Stevens or George Goethals, McCullough describes the West Indian laborer as "soft-spoken, courteous, sober, very religious." Almost all were illiterate, he says, thus ignoring the fact that a high proportion had acquired some education and could read and write. McCullough's treatment of health care provides a useful example of his approach. He begins by noting that the Caribbean laborers suffered more from disease and sickness than did white Americans. He reprints nearly two pages of James A. Williams's harrowing account of sickness and hospitalization from Box 25. Then McCullough ends by reporting the official statistic that deaths during the construction decade amounted to less than 5,000 and that it was a "miracle of medical progress" that Williams survived. The tone focuses overall on the triumphant achievements of Zonian medical care.[15]

McCullough's use of the testimonies, in short, brings to mind Michel-Rolph Trouillot's observation that even primary sources contesting official narratives can be used in ways that reinforce the hegemonic interpretations.

Thirty years after *The Path Between the Seas* appeared, British nonfiction writer Matthew Parker published *Panama Fever: The Epic Story of the Building of the Panama Canal*. Like McCullough's book, *Panama Fever* begins with the French project and takes the story through to its completion by the United States. As his title suggests, Parker frames his story similarly to McCullough's: it is indeed an epic tale, filled with stories of "The French Tragedy," as part 2 of the book is titled, and then, in part 3, "The American Triumph." Parker likewise focuses great attention on the politicians, diplomats, and officials who led the project, and devotes many pages to the engineering, technological, and medical innovations. Like McCullough, Parker is an excellent writer, and he tells a rousing tale. However, Parker provides more helpful information on the social experiences of people in the zone, and this includes more—and more effective—exploration of the lives of Afro-Caribbeans. He makes much more use of the testimonies in Box 25 and complements them with new sources that illuminate the lives of Black workers—most notably the personal papers of British consul Claude Mallet.[16] His interpretation of race and racism is more sophisticated and compelling than McCullough's as well. In discussing the relative absence of overt protests by Black Caribbeans, Parker astutely explores the role of zone police in disciplining laborers as well as the surplus of their labor on the isthmus. He interviewed an "old-timer" who noted that inclinations toward protest were also hampered by laborers' need for money and their sheer exhaustion after a long day of work. As compared to McCullough's apologetic comment that this was "not entirely" racial injustice, Parker is much clearer and notes the vast-shaping influence of racial discrimination across the zone. Black Caribbeans' experiences are not limited primarily to ten pages of one chapter but instead receive treatment throughout the book. If Parker's portrayal of Black Caribbeans fails to break completely with officials' view of them, he nonetheless comes closer to granting them their full humanity and complexity than McCullough does.

We can contrast mass market explorations like McCullough's and Parker's with accounts by scholars of Latin America and the Caribbean. Latin Americanist Michael Conniff generated more scholarly interest in Black Caribbeans' labor on the isthmus with his classic 1985 study *Black Labor on a White Canal: Panama, 1904–1981*. The beginning chapter on the construction era provides a brief but skillful exploration of challenges Black workers confronted as well as conditions on home islands that prompted them to leave. It makes some limited use of the Box 25 testimonies, but Conniff's major concern was the development of policy and the spread of the gold and silver segregation system.[17] Another early effort to focus on Black Caribbean labor in the Canal Zone came from Lancelot Lewis, with a short dissertation completed at Tulane University and published in 1980 as *The West Indian in Panama*. Lewis's work relied extensively on the testimonies in Box 25 and reprinted many of them along with other primary sources that illuminated the experiences of Caribbean workers. Yet his very short thesis repeated many age-old assumptions about Caribbean workers, for example, that they were quite passive in the face of racial injustice and that they were predominantly unskilled workers.[18] Nonetheless, Lewis's focus on Black Caribbean laborers would prove generative to future scholars. Similarly in the early 1980s two additional books appeared that created better understanding of, and interest in, West Indian labor in the Canal Zone: George W. Westerman's *Los Immigrantes Antillanos en Panamá* and Velma Newton's *The Silver Men: West Indian Labour Migration to Panama 1850–19.*[19] With each of these books, the reader receives a more complete picture of Black Caribbeans' world. Both were more sociological than historical in their methodologies, enumerating the salaries, education, medical care, and so on that West Indians shared. Westerman makes no use of the testimonies in Box 25, and Newton provides only scarce passages from the competition.

A more recent book provides by far the most eloquent and comprehensive exploration of Black Caribbeans' labor on the isthmus and, as well, makes superb use of the testimonies in Box 25. *Dying to Better Themselves* by the Jamaican novelist and poet Olive Senior, published in 2014, traces Black workers' lives on the isthmus from the building of the mid-nineteenth-century railroad to the aftermath of the US canal construction project. Most of the book focuses on the US construction effort. This is a magisterial work, more inclusive and probing than any previous study of Caribbean workers' life and labor on the isthmus.

Senior came of age in a Jamaican household full of people who had "gone to Panama." A grandfather and two of his siblings had spent time there. The grandfather died before Senior was born, and she had no knowledge of his experiences on the isthmus. Nonetheless she grew up having heard about the struggles of those who traveled to Panama, as well as the men and women who returned with Panama money. "This book represents both a search for and a tribute to the composite 'grandfather': the legendary forefather who vanished, or who came home crippled, as well as the one who brought home 'Panama gold' and used it to better himself."[20] Senior noted that many works on the canal had focused on the engineering and medical innovations. She knew she had to "tell our story"—"the canal's most essential tale: that of the men and women whose physical labour made it a reality." Furthermore, she intended "to let the voices of those workers speak for themselves alongside the official accounts."[21] Her goal was to tell the story of the Panama Canal from "the underside," focused on the laborers and the impact of the project on their home islands.[22]

Senior achieves a more complex portrayal of West Indians on the isthmus, perhaps due to her personal connections as well as skills as a writer and researcher. She mined a wide range of sources for information on Black Caribbeans' lives—from Jamaican and US archives to government reports, to contemporary memoirs and journalism, to oral sources including interviews she conducted in the 1970s. Because she combines her reading of the testimonies in Box 25 with other sources, she skillfully puts them in context. Her knowledge of West Indian experiences—especially of the male workers—is deep and broad, and this enables her to cover aspects of their history rarely explored by other scholars, such as inter-island rivalries, for example. As a scholar of literature, she makes excellent use of novels, short stories, poetry, and songs to illuminate Caribbean lives and labor. Her extensive knowledge is matched by an eloquent writing style that brings a poetic quality to the book. Discussing the long history of Caribbeans migrating beyond their home islands for work from the mid-nineteenth century onward, for example, Senior concludes, "In many ways the impact of these movements on the home societies reverberates still, as if the Panama Railroad had set in motion a ghost train that has never stopped, still carrying West Indian wanderers far beyond the confines of their countries so that today, more West Indians live abroad than at home, many pushed and pulled by the same factors that were operating in 1850."[23]

Like Olive Senior, the historian Joan Flores-Villalobos makes eloquent use of the testimonies in Box 25 but places them within the context of many other sources on Black Caribbean workers. Her study *The Silver Women: How Black Women's Labor Made the Panama Canal*, as the title suggests, does not focus on the male workers who wrote almost all of the competition entries. Yet Flores deploys the testimonies by men to portray the larger context of life and labor on the canal. And the one woman who wrote an evocative account of her journey to Panama becomes the occasion for a stirring discussion by Flores. She explains how Mrs. Mary Couloote traveled to Panama, like many Caribbean women, independently rather than as a contracted laborer. Her difficult journey, as a storm hit the ship and caused the death of five

Jamaicans, allows Flores to bring the difficult passage of Caribbeans to life. She makes use of Box 25 to portray the threat of both death and injury male workers faced, but she also skillfully detects critical pieces of information about women's roles from the mostly male writers. For example, one worker's entry discusses female tradeswomen, or higglers. Another worker, Alfred Dottin, notes that "I had to learn how to cook by force and wash my clothes because of the scarcity of women."[24]

As this mapping of the historiography shows, scholars have increasingly focused attention on the world of Caribbean canal workers in recent years. At the same time, new explorations have emerged as well from filmmakers, Afro-Caribbean descendants, and librarians and archivists. Together they are not only keeping the world of the canal builders alive but also creating new archives that generate significant insights into their experiences.

Roman Foster and his 1985 film *The Diggers* bring together many of these themes. Born in Panama to a family of Caribbean descent, his two grand-fathers having worked to build the canal, Foster grew up hearing stories of the construction years. As an elementary school boy, he would walk slowly with his grandfather when he visited another aged canal builder friend. They would sit out on the porch and tell stories that, Foster said, stayed with him his entire life. Years later, having moved to the United States and earning degrees in history from Brooklyn College and the State University of New York at Stony Brook, Foster got to know the writer Alex Haley and began telling him stories of the construction project. Haley encouraged him to gather stories from canal workers still living. And so began a major project.[25] Foster managed to get a list of all the living canal builders from the US government and traveled across their diaspora to interview them, beginning in the 1970s. He described the experience of talking with the aged canal builders, calling it a turning point in his life. The emotions expressed during interviews moved him profoundly. "There's nothing more touching than to see an 80, 85, 90-year-old individual, crying. And here I am, how am I going to react this. But as I asked, why are you crying, they all said the same thing. . . . NOBODY has ever come to me and asked me, what happened in Panama. Nobody."

After conducting and analyzing many interviews, Foster decided to make a film. With support from the Ford Foundation and other organizations, he identified surviving canal workers who seemed especially eloquent, based on the interviews he had conducted, and traveled to Panama with a film crew. His film *The Diggers* premiered on PBS in 1985. Over the course of ninety minutes, the film tells the story of the construction project, splicing together period footage with interviews with canal workers. It is powerful to see these men in their eighties and nineties explaining the challenges they experienced. Workers described how they felt upon being excluded from the commissary for gold workers and being refused access to white drinking fountains. Yet as one man declared, "I didn't let the discrimination take hold of me." At an event at the University of Florida, Foster concluded his comments about the film, declaring, "This was our way of paying tribute to the builders of the Panama Canal." He also noted the lingering sense among Afro-Caribbeans that they are not yet fully accepted in Panama. *The Diggers*, Foster said, has been shown all over the world—except in Panama. He met with the president of Panama and encouraged a showing of the film but was declined. "I left that Presidential Palace with my heart flat."

More recently, two filmmakers in Panama discovered the dramatic history of the Caribbean canal builders. The 2015 documentary film by Delfina Vidal and Mercedes Arias, *Box 25: The Untold Story of the Panama Canal*, focused on the testimonies held at the Library of Congress as a way to explore the building of the canal and the troubled relationship between Panama and the United States. Delfina Vidal, noting that she is the daughter and granddaughter of librarians, describes her surprise upon discovering the testimonies in Box 25. The film tells the story of the "marriage" of Panama and the United States upon the latter's acquisition of the Panama Canal Zone in 1903, and their final divorce in 1999 when the canal became the property of the Republic of Panama. It notes how certain voices and stories—like those of Caribbean canal workers—have been lost, and the filmmakers use live readings and animated drawings to bring to life the experiences of canal workers. Without using the word colonialism, they clearly note the unequal power relationship between the two countries. Jorge Quijano, the chief administrator of the Panama Canal, comments that during the nearly 100 years of US control over the Canal Zone, Panamanians "had to cross through another country to reach parts of our own country." The filmmakers ask the question, Why do these crucial documents reside in a vault in the United States? They assert that the documents should be held by the Republic of Panama. Upon visiting the originals at the Library of Congress, Mercedes Arias notes that she felt she was looking at a family album. "They were my photos, but they were not in Panama."[26]

Meanwhile, a pathbreaking collaboration between descendants of canal workers across the Caribbean-Panamanian diaspora and librarians and archivists at the University of Florida is creating a model of community-based archival creation and preservation. Descendants of Caribbean canal builders in Panama and across the Caribbean and the United States have worked with the Digital Library of the Caribbean and the George Smathers Library at the University of Florida to create a phenomenal collection of materials related to the canal. Descendants' activism has been crucial in pushing for the creation of this archive, as has been the commitment of librarians and archivists. Their collaboration included the digitization of the testimonies in Box 25, for example, which had originally been available only at the Library of Congress or a typescript copy held at the Afro-Antillean Museum of Panama.

The story of this collaboration begins with Frances Williams-Yearwood, who grew up in the Canal Zone to a family of Jamaican and Barbadian descent. Williams-Yearwood's grandparents moved to the Canal Zone in the early twentieth century and worked for the Isthmian Canal Commission. When Williams-Yearwood was sixteen, she moved with her family to the United States, where she has lived ever since. Yet she has remained connected to the West Indian community in Panama and visits family there often. In 2016 she made a journey to her father's grave at Corozal and, she says, "had an epiphany." Surveying the cemetery landscape, the graves covered in high grasses, and the dilapidation of the grounds, it seemed a sad testament to the place of the West Indian community in Panama broadly speaking. Speaking with Williams-Yearwood via Zoom, I watched tears come to her eyes as she described that day: "I realized who I am today is the result of a community. I couldn't believe what I saw. It looked like a total disrespect to me."[27]

So Williams-Yearwood took action. She "reached out to the diaspora," as she puts it, and people responded. Online chat rooms and newsletters became a venue for connecting Williams-Yearwood to wide-ranging descendants of those buried in the cemeteries. A team came together and began pushing the Panamanian government to improve the cemetery at Corozal. In 2017 Williams-Yearwood and others founded an organization, the Cemetery Preservation Foundation (CGM), to improve and preserve the Corozal, Gatun, and Mt. Hope cemeteries. Noting that the white cemeteries had been meticulously preserved, they created an Adopt-A-Grave program to uncover and preserve the burial sites of Afro-Caribbeans. Soon they had repaired some 700 (of approximately 26,000 total) at Corozal. As the website of the CGM declares, "What should be a place where families come to pay tribute has turned into a deplorable domicile unfitting of the legacy these workers deserve. CGM is dedicated to ensuring the maintenance of these sites [is] upheld in a manner in which they deserve."[28]

In 2019 Williams-Yearwood decided to attend the Panama Canal Society Reunion in Orlando, Florida, to publicize the work of her Cemetery Preservation Foundation. The Panama Canal Society is an organization of US government employees who helped construct or maintain the Panama Canal. Its website notes, "Our principles and purposes shall be allegiance, or respect, to the United States of America, fidelity to our by-laws, and preservation of ideals and friendships formed while working in the Canal Zone or the Republic of Panama." The society founded the Panama Canal Museum in Seminole, Florida, in 1998. Both the society and the museum reflect the interests and experiences of the predominantly white US community in the Canal Zone. In 2012 the Panama Canal Museum closed and its vast collection, including more than 12,000 objects and millions of pages of documents, was transferred to become the Panama Canal Museum Collection at the University of Florida's George Smathers Library—itself already a leading repository of Latin American and Caribbean archival materials.[29] Archivists at UF from the beginning knew they would need to work to make the Panama Canal Museum Collection reflect the experiences of West Indians on the Isthmus of Panama, as well as the white US "Zonians."

In 2019 when Frances Williams-Yearwood visited the Panama Canal Society Reunion, UF archivists John Nemmers and Elizabeth Bemis were hosting a special exhibition of materials from the Panama Canal Museum Collection related to Operation Just Cause—the military code name for the US invasion of Panama in 1989 to depose President Manuel Noriega. As Williams-Yearwood examined the posters and memorabilia, she remembered thinking "gosh, there's nothing here that looks like me!" She introduced herself to Elizabeth ("Betsy") Bemis and complimented the exhibition. Yet she also told them, "It seems like it's a one-sided story. I don't see anything here that looks like the community I grew up in. And Betsy explained she was from the University of Florida, and they inherited this collection from the Americans." Williams-Yearwood spoke at length with curators Betsy Bemis and John Nemmers and learned that they shared her desire to build the collection's holdings related to West Indians.

So once again Frances Williams-Yearwood "reached out to the diaspora." Ten individuals from across the United States and Panama flew to Gainesville, Florida, in September 2019 to meet with the archivists and scholars at UF. They spoke with the archivists about the ways the West Indian community within and beyond Panama has felt marginalized and their contributions to the canal's construction and operations minimized or erased. From these meetings emerged a partnership between the CGM activists and the UF library to collect oral history interviews, artifacts, and documents from the West Indian diaspora. The CGM created a new division within its organization, the Pan Caribbean Sankofa (PCS), to focus the work of its collaboration with the University of Florida. The latter supports PCS's work financially, while the leaders of PCS are responsible for networking among the Afro-Caribbean-Panamanian diaspora and conducting the oral histories—which then join the UF library's holdings for preservation and accessibility. According to Williams-Yearwood they are trying to work fast and gather interviews with the older generations before they pass away. PCS has conducted so far approximately fifty interviews, of which nearly thirty are available for viewing at the UF George Smathers Library website.[30]

The collaboration is an inspiring model of community-generated archival production. But it did not emerge easily and the tensions the archivists and community activists had to navigate through are instructive as well. Both Williams-Yearwood and archivist Betsy Bemis have commented that a great many issues had to be worked out, and the process involved a lot of debate. According to Williams-Yearwood, the biggest tension involved the shape of the organization they should create and who should control it. Some of the original group members wanted to create a new, independent museum or archive to house the materials they would generate—something similar to the Afro-Antillean Museum in Panama City. As curator Betsy Bemis has explained, some original attendees opted not to continue participating; of those, some believed the West Indian community should manage its own materials, and others decided that an institution in the United States could not be trusted to preserve them correctly.[31]

Williams-Yearwood thought rejecting the collaboration with the University of Florida library would be foolhardy, and she rejected the idea that a "white institution" could not be trusted to preserve West Indian materials. The tensions, she commented in a conversation via Zoom, reflected divisions within the Caribbean-Panamanian diaspora itself. Older and younger generations see things differently, as do those who lived in the zone versus in the cities of Panama, or even those on the Atlantic or Pacific side of the country. For her part, Williams-Yearwood thought a carefully constructed partnership with UF, one that gave her team control over conducting the oral histories but benefitted from the knowledge and financial support of UF, would be the best path forward. The original team of ten who had flown to Gainesville for the initial meeting dwindled down to four as some members objected to the plan. But for those who continued, the partnership has flowered into a powerful engine for generating and preserving materials and memories of the Afro-Caribbean world in Panama.[32]

Other projects have likewise connected canal worker descendants to the University of Florida. As news of the collaboration with PCS spread, new discoveries led to a range of exciting projects. Emilio Collins, a descendant of Panamanian Afro-Antilleans, realized that the Panama Canal Museum Collection's offering of high school yearbooks included none from West Indian schools. He began a project to remedy that. So far, Collins has been responsible for the donation of fifteen digital copies of Afro-Antillean yearbooks to the UF library system.[33] Another fascinating digital humanities project developed from the donation of a notebook kept by Enid Hall, who had grown up in the silver town of La Boca. In the 1950s the US government relocated the thousands of residents and turned La Boca into a white US citizen town. Enid Hall's notebook made it possible to recreate the original silver town in great detail, which led to a project at UF to bring the town to life digitally.[34]

The spirit of collaboration pervades all of these projects. Pan Caribbean Sankofa and the University of Florida Panama Canal Museum Collection have cohosted several events that bring together librarians, scholars, and descendants to explore the ongoing work. As curator Betsy Bemis stated during one, the archivists' focus is on supporting the creation of materials by Afro-Caribbean Panamanians. "Our goal is to let the community's voices speak for themselves."[35] Thanks to the determined labors of descendants and the expert support provided by UF librarians and archivists, the world of Afro-Caribbean Panamanians has become accessible to new generations.

These are important developments for the entire Afro-Caribbean diaspora but perhaps nowhere more so than in Panama itself. Arcelio Hartley, one of the descendant activists working with PCS, lives in Panama City and shared with me his concerns about both the continued racism Afro-Caribbeans confront in Panama and the diminution of their culture.[36] He noted fights that have had to occur even now over Afro-Caribbean children in schools banned from sporting certain hairstyles or clothing. Similarly, he described activists' recent struggle to pass a law requiring that Black history be taught in the schools. Hartley also expressed his worries that West Indian traditions are being lost. Younger people in Afro-Caribbean Panamanian households are now less likely to learn English and thus are less connected to their Caribbean roots. Xenophobia in Panama has itself pushed many Black Panamanians to embrace the Spanish language and culture, and as a result they lose touch with Caribbean traditions. Such concerns motivate Hartley to work with PCS conducting interviews. In addition he is the president of one of the most important organizations working to preserve Afro-Caribbean memories and culture in Panama—the Society of Friends of the Afro-Antillean Museum of Panama, or SAMAAP (La Sociedad de Amigos del Museo Afroantilleano de Panama). Their museum is housed in a historic building built by Barbadian workers more than 110 years ago. It originally served as the Christian Mission Church for the West Indian community. The museum was founded in 1980 and is owned by the Panamanian government, but SAMAAP has been critical in supporting it and expanding its holdings. The small building holds historic photographs and recreates a typical West Indian living room with furniture and other artifacts. Outside the museum is a beautiful mural stretching alongside the entryway to the museum and depicting the culture and history of West Indians on the isthmus. SAMAAP also sponsors an annual Afro-Antillean festival in Panama and a range of other cultural and academic activities to promote awareness of the community's history.

Hartley's devotion to strengthening Afro-Caribbean culture in Panama is linked to his own family's history. He is the third generation of Panama Canal workers, with grandparents on both sides having traveled from Jamaica to work on the canal. Both his father and paternal grandfather worked for the Panama Railroad. Hartley himself worked as towboat master and then manager of the transit operations division for forty-six years. Between himself and his father and grandfathers, the family counts more than 100 years of labor for the Panama Canal. Like Frances Williams-Yearwood, Arcelio Hartley is a prime example of the work descendants are doing to preserve the memory and culture of Afro-Caribbeans on the Isthmus of Panama.

This exploration of depictions of the original Afro-Caribbean canal builders uncovers a great many changes since the accounts by government officials and tourists written in the early twentieth century. More complex understandings of class and race—due to the impact of the civil rights movement and transformations in the ways historians research and interpret the past, for example—have encouraged a more sophisticated scholarly treatment of West Indians' history. The first-person accounts in Box 25 must be given credit as well. The West Indian laborers who authored their testimonies for the competition articulated their own visions of life and work on the canal and thus helped shift perspectives away from the exoticizing and marginalizing approaches of earlier decades. By centering our understanding on how the workers experienced their lives, Box 25 helped reframe historical understandings. At the same time, an analysis of historians' use of Box 25 reminds us that even first-person accounts can be used to reinforce racialized, colonialist, and top-down depictions of Black Caribbean workers. This is particularly a problem if there is little understanding of the degree to which the authors of testimonies do or do not reflect the experiences of the tens of thousands of other workers. In other words, assessing the origins and character of the source becomes essential for an accurate interpretation. The work of scholars like Olive Senior and Joan Flores-Villalobos to place the testimonies within the larger context of sources on Caribbean workers enables them to illuminate the West Indian experience on the Isthmus of Panama more fully. Meanwhile the work of pioneering filmmaker Roman Foster and a generation of thoughtful descendants in the Afro-Caribbean Panamanian community like Frances Williams-Yearwood and Arcelio Hartley provide hopeful examples of new archives emerging that capture canal workers' world in their own words.

Conclusion
Silences That Speak

The workers of Box 25 are silent now, having passed away one by one in the late twentieth century. Edgar Simmons, called "Shine" by his bosses, died from septicemia in November 1963 — soon after having composed his moving testimony for the Isthmian Historical Society competition. Jeremiah Waisome, who arrived on the isthmus from Nicaragua as a boy, moved to the United States to live with his daughter after retirement and died at the Jewish Hospital of Brooklyn in December 1972, aged 72. Barbadian Harrigan Austin died from complications of bronchitis at the Gorgas Hospital in 1976, aged 89. Robert Chambers, who arrived from Jamaica, died in 1970 from heart disease at the age of 84.

Constantine Parkinson continued working for the Panama Canal Commission until he retired from active duty in 1957. He lived another thirty-two years, making do with the modest disability payments from the US government. In 1983 he wrote a note of thanks to the Panama Canal Commission: "I deeply appreciate your always help to we the canal old timers. . . . I thank you with gratitude for getting me a new wheelchair with better convenience to suit my two artificial legs." He remained active, serving as representative for the Atlantic side of Cash Relief Pensioners.[1] In 1987 Parkinson requested that his granddaughter Lucia Dreck de Ortega be issued power of attorney as he could no longer pick up his disability checks. He died on December 29, 1989, from an abdominal aneurism at the age of 95.[2]

These workers had lived through an age of wonder, watching the Isthmus of Panama become transformed through the efforts of the US government along with their own arduous labor. We first met Constantine Parkinson when, as the son of Jamaicans who had worked on the French canal construction effort in the 1880s, he got his first job with the Isthmian Canal Commission at the age of fifteen. We learned of the accident that led to amputation of his leg when he was only nineteen years old, and then his fight to be rehired by the Isthmian Canal Commission despite the crippling accident. He assertively demanded continued treatment and new and improved artificial legs from the US government during the next decades. Over the years he worked as a telephone attendant, a switch tender, a helper responsible for issuing

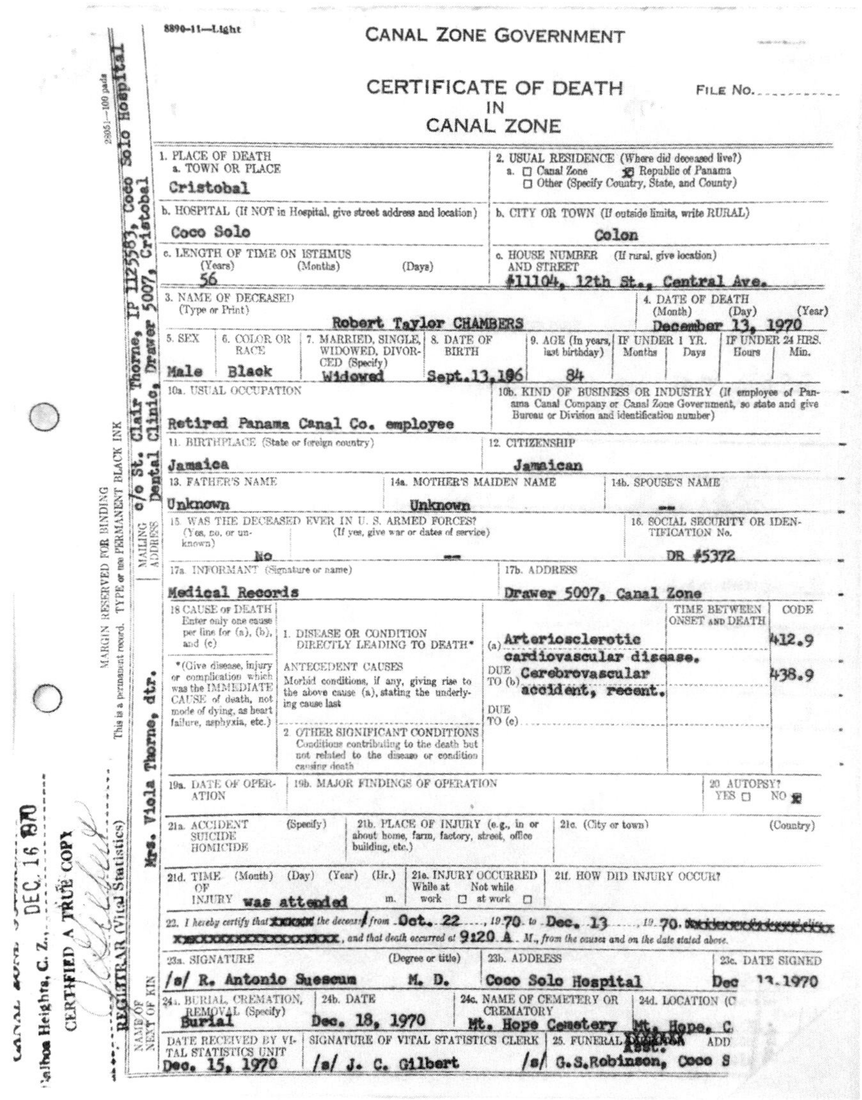

CANAL ZONE GOVERNMENT

CERTIFICATE OF DEATH
IN
CANAL ZONE

FILE No. _____

Left margin (vertical text):
IF 112558?, Coco Solo Hospital
c/o St. Clair Thorne, Drawer 5007, Cristobal
Dental Clinic,
MAILING ADDRESS
MARGIN RESERVED FOR BINDING   TYPE or use PERMANENT BLACK INK   This is a permanent record.

Mrs. Viola Thorne, dtr.

REGISTRAR (Vital Statistics)   NAME OF NEXT OF KIN
CANAL ZONE GOVERNMENT   Balboa Heights, C. Z.   DEC. 16 1970
CERTIFIED A TRUE COPY

1. PLACE OF DEATH
a. TOWN OR PLACE
Cristobal

b. HOSPITAL (If NOT in Hospital, give street address and location)
Coco Solo

c. LENGTH OF TIME ON ISTHMUS
(Years) **56** (Months) (Days)

2. USUAL RESIDENCE (Where did deceased live?)
a. ☐ Canal Zone ☒ Republic of Panama
☐ Other (Specify Country, State, and County)

b. CITY OR TOWN (If outside limits, write RURAL)
Colon

c. HOUSE NUMBER AND STREET (If rural, give location)
#11104, 12th St., Central Ave.

3. NAME OF DECEASED (Type or Print)
Robert Taylor CHAMBERS

4. DATE OF DEATH (Month) (Day) (Year)
December 13, 1970

5. SEX **Male**
6. COLOR OR RACE **Black**
7. MARRIED, SINGLE, WIDOWED, DIVORCED (Specify) **Widowed**
8. DATE OF BIRTH **Sept. 13, 196**
9. AGE (In years, last birthday) **84** | IF UNDER 1 YR. Months Days | IF UNDER 24 HRS. Hours Min.

10a. USUAL OCCUPATION
Retired Panama Canal Co. employee

10b. KIND OF BUSINESS OR INDUSTRY (If employee of Panama Canal Company or Canal Zone Government, so state and give Bureau or Division and identification number)

11. BIRTHPLACE (State or foreign country)
Jamaica

12. CITIZENSHIP
Jamaican

13. FATHER'S NAME
Unknown

14a. MOTHER'S MAIDEN NAME
Unknown

14b. SPOUSE'S NAME
--

15. WAS THE DECEASED EVER IN U. S. ARMED FORCES? (Yes, no, or unknown)
No
(If yes, give war or dates of service) **--**

16. SOCIAL SECURITY OR IDENTIFICATION No.
DR #5372

17a. INFORMANT (Signature or name)
Medical Records

17b. ADDRESS
Drawer 5007, Canal Zone

18. CAUSE OF DEATH
Enter only one cause per line for (a), (b), and (c)

(Give disease, injury or complication which was the IMMEDIATE CAUSE of death, not mode of dying, as heart failure, asphyxia, etc.)

1. DISEASE OR CONDITION DIRECTLY LEADING TO DEATH*
(a) **Arteriosclerotic cardiovascular disease.**

ANTECEDENT CAUSES
Morbid conditions, if any, giving rise to the above cause (a), stating the underlying cause last
DUE TO (b) **Cerebrovascular accident, recent.**
DUE TO (c)

2. OTHER SIGNIFICANT CONDITIONS
Conditions contributing to the death but not related to the disease or condition causing death

	TIME BETWEEN ONSET AND DEATH	CODE
(a)		412.9
(b)		438.9

19a. DATE OF OPERATION

19b. MAJOR FINDINGS OF OPERATION

20. AUTOPSY? YES ☐ NO ☒

21a. ACCIDENT SUICIDE HOMICIDE (Specify)

21b. PLACE OF INJURY (e.g., in or about home, farm, factory, street, office building, etc.)

21c. (City or town)

21c. (Country)

21d. TIME OF INJURY (Month) (Day) (Year) (Hr.) m.

21e. INJURY OCCURRED While at work ☐ Not while at work ☐

21f. HOW DID INJURY OCCUR?
was attended

22. I hereby certify that ~~xxxxx~~ the deceased from **Oct. 22**, 19 **70** to **Dec. 13**, 19 **70**. ~~xxxxxxxxxxxxxxxxxx~~, and that death occurred at **9:20 A** M., from the causes and on the date stated above.

23a. SIGNATURE
/s/ R. Antonio Suescum

(Degree or title) **M. D.**

23b. ADDRESS
Coco Solo Hospital

23c. DATE SIGNED
Dec 13, 1970

24a. BURIAL, CREMATION, REMOVAL (Specify)
Burial

24b. DATE **Dec. 18, 1970**

24c. NAME OF CEMETERY OR CREMATORY **Mt. Hope Cemetery**

24d. LOCATION (City) **Mt. Hope, C.**

DATE RECEIVED BY VITAL STATISTICS UNIT
Dec. 15, 1970

SIGNATURE OF VITAL STATISTICS CLERK
/s/ J. C. Gilbert

25. FUNERAL DIRECTOR
/s/ G. S. Robinson, Coco S

FIGURE C.1 Robert Chambers's death certificate, National Personnel Records Center

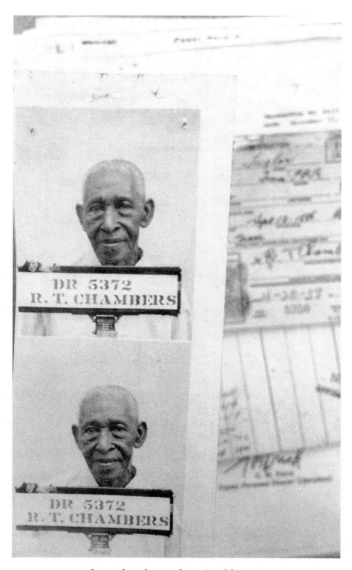

FIGURE C.2 Robert Chambers, photo in older age,
National Personnel Records Center

tools, a watchman, and an interpreter for customs and police officers. He volunteered for a variety of community programs and worked as steward and head of the recreation committee for the American Federation of State, County and Municipal Employees' Local 900.[3]

Constantine Parkinson was one of the last of the original canal builders to pass away. He lived a longer life than many, but in other respects his final years shared key characteristics with others. Some felt bitter that their final decades were so challenging. As Z. H. McKenzie wrote, "The wage scale during the Canal Construction was So Small that we could not put by any Saving in the Bank, hence the majority of ous left empty handed. To lived or die. of which many died from a weak heart." Yet others shared in the pride felt by Samuel Smith: "My greatest experience was the construction of the Panama Canal, and I am more than proud to be among the many old timers who have helped so willingly in giving a hand in building this masterpiece."[4]

In writing up their experiences for the Isthmian Historical Society competition, these "old-timers" created a living record that allows their voices to be heard today. Borrowing from Michel-Rolph Trouillot, we should note that the writers of Box 25 were people inhabiting three capacities. They were simultaneously occupants of structural positions as Black West Indian workers living amid British and US imperialism; actors interacting within that larger context; and subjects — in other words "voices aware of their vocality."[5] Considering the lessons and secrets held in Box 25 requires that we be cognizant of these three different positions the writers occupied. In this book we have traced their lives, from their youth on islands across the Caribbean and countries of Latin America, confronting British colonialism in most cases, to their migrations and diasporic-world-making, to their interactions with the highly regimented power of the US empire in the Canal Zone and the complex and often xenophobic society of the Republic of Panama. They labored on the canal not only during the construction era but for decades after, along the way witnessing challenges to US colonialism and Black struggles for equality in both the Canal Zone and Panama.

The history constructed in Box 25 was produced by a distinct group of actors. These were almost entirely male canal workers who lived exceptional lives. Unlike the vast majority of canal construction workers, they continued working on the canal for decades rather than migrating onward to plantations across Central America, or returning home, or traveling onward to Cuba or New York City. We have seen that they were not the diggers and dynamiters often imagined as the quintessential canal builders. Rather these men achieved significant occupational mobility and worked at jobs requiring some skill and a level of responsibility. Their writing stresses their struggles to achieve occupational mobility, changing their jobs often to find a better position—one less dangerous, or better paying, or with a kinder foreman. These men remained in the orbit of the United States and its power for the rest of their lives. And they also engaged with the world of Panama itself. Even if they lived in the Canal Zone with its strong sense of white American hierarchy, Panamanian culture and politics also shaped their lives in complex ways. And so over the decades the struggles of Afro-Caribbeans against racism and xenophobia in both Panama and the Canal Zone were likely, to some degree, their struggles as well. Understanding this distinctive positionality of the Box 25 writers is necessary to grasp the secrets held within their testimonies.

Box 25 constructs a history that challenges the US government's narrative in important ways. Most striking, perhaps, is the sense they articulate of their pain, fears, and struggles during the construction years. They wrote at length about the dangers they faced on the job from disease, accidents, and dynamite explosions. A palpable feeling that death surrounded them appears constantly in their writing. The indifference of white officials to the workers' plight added insult to injury. According to Barbadian Clifford Hunt, "Men in my gang tell the boss I am going out to ease my bowels and they die in the bush and nobody look for you." In a powerful statement Aaron Clarke described the different jobs he carried out in the Canal Zone. "I dug ditches dropped mosquito oil made drains dug graves acted as pall bearer and sometimes when we could afford the time I performed a short religious ceremony." The need for spirituality and religion was great; that it was left to a gravedigger to provide spiritual comfort is telling.

Perhaps death being so ever-present led to greater reliance on faith and religion. Thoughts of god enter often into the testimonies. There are common sayings: as Samuel A. Smith, who worked as an oiler on a dredge put it, "We must say thanks to God in helping to make this wonder a success." Many of the testimonies end with a similar expression of gratefulness to god. Others discuss their faith in god as helping them survive disasters and disease. Jeremiah Waisome described riding on a labor train when a dead-end track had been left open. The train was moving at a high speed with ten cars attached. Many workers were killed—"one could hear the moaning and hollering that morning it was awful." But "God was with me that morning." Those who missed disaster often felt god and prayers were responsible for their good luck. One writer described the reaction when the first airplane was sighted in 1907. "Some thought it was judgement coming from God upon the land, and they began to pray."[6] Amos Parks stressed that they all went to church on Sundays. "In those days People take Church more serious than today, maybe because in construction days the amount of West Indians that lose their lives on the job was mournful to talk about. . . . In those days you see today and tomorrow you are a dead man. You had to pray everyday for God to carry you safe and bring you back." As George Westerman has pointed out, the church was the most important social institution supporting canal workers during the construction days.[7]

The testimonies also contrast with both the government's narrative and, until recently, scholarship on the canal's history, by stressing the racism they faced. The almighty power and racial condescension of white US officials and foremen comes through powerfully. When Jeremiah Waisome innocently corrected a foreman who called him by the wrong name, he got called the insulting N-word and was told never to speak that way to a white man again.[8] Even amid the deferential tone of many testimonies, their awareness and resentment of the racism they faced comes through clearly.

One of the most powerful aspects of the testimonies is the opportunity they provided to follow the writers to the end of their lives. The ways they express their struggle with aging, particularly when combined with information gleaned from the personnel records, brings their lives before us in full three-dimensionality. They wrote of their eyesight declining, their sicknesses, and their need for more help from the government. Mixed with such complaints was an awareness of the epic work they had done and their disgruntled feeling of being unappreciated. Clifford Hunt of Cristobal declared, "I cry sometime to see how I put this Canal through up to [now] they don't pay us no mine today men are walking in and have everything sweet. . . . We are dying for starvation but I ask God to open all you hearts and have mercy on us."[9]

Although Ruth Stuhl framed her search as one for the "Best True Stories of Life and Work" during the construction of the Panama Canal, in fact the writers focused almost entirely on their work lives. In this focus on the job, many aspects of life became buried or silenced. Understanding these workers as agents of history requires examining the quiet bits, the matters left unsaid or provided only in fragments, as well as the emphatic declarations. For example, we know from scholarship on Caribbeans in Panama that maintaining ties to family and communities on their home islands was very important, but one sees few references to that in the testimonies. Those who mention the issue do so because they feel it is a problem. Workers struggled to save enough money to send some home and help families there. They worried over how to keep that money safe, often tying the cash to their bodies because they didn't trust the banks. Several men talked about the effort to save money so they could return home and make a show of their success; others discussed busily sending money orders home to family after pay day.[10] The pressure to make money to impress people when they returned home was real. And some felt they had no family left back home. Albert Banister noted, "Why you did not go home Banister respectiful I answered Mam I would glad to go home but I can't go home empty handed first all of my relative is dead nobody know me at home I am a perfect stranger no friends no family they all dead out."[11] There is a sad melancholy in Banister's comment which must have been shared by others.

When workers turned their attention to life beyond the job, a few themes stood out. One was food: they would list the prices of different requisite food items but also discuss their hunger, their desire for good food—and their disgust at the food provided by the US government. Joseph H. Fox noted the cafeteria food was so bad, "sometime we look on the food and leave it the same place on the table cannot be eaten." Likewise the carpenter John Butcher described his dinner in the mess hall: there was a "meal of cooked rice which was hard enough to shoot deers, sauce spread all over the rice, and a slab of meat which many men either spent an hour trying to chew or eventually throw away because it was too hard." In the early years, one man commented, the government food wasn't hot, but they weren't allowed to cook their own. After a few years this became possible, and there was a mass flight away from the government cafeterias. Food gradually became more plentiful—popping up in the testimonies are memories of buying a ham on payday and eating it all week, or gratitude for the government providing the men with ice cream.[12]

One of the most common themes in the testimonies—other than the prevalence of death and disease—was the sense of how difficult conditions were in the early years, and how much they improved over time. And this in turn hinged significantly on the absence or presence of women. Many men mentioned how difficult life was initially because there were no women to help them. Alfred Dottin noted, "I had to learn to cook by force and wash my own clothes because of the scarcity of women in the Empire section of the Canal, where I lived." Another man noted that women were as hard to find as "hen's teeth." And Jules LeCurrieux eloquently described the difference women made: "So just think of the life of the pioneers of this Big Ditch the West Indian Nigger of the 1903 to 1908 gang. Now here comes a little improvement, the West Indian Negro woman began to immigrate here, then the poor old bastards found themselves wives of their tribes, and began to live like human beings and not beasts, or slaves, they found someone to cook them a decent meal, to wash their clothes, someone to be a companion, and then to find a clean and decent place to sleep, and started a new generation of West Indian Panamanians." With his comment, LeCurrieux identified the critical role Caribbean women would come to play in a range of social reproduction activities as well as community building. One of the other rare comments regarding women came from Harrigan Austin, who noted that life was so difficult, the government brought women from Martinique for the men.[13]

Remarkably, there are few references to women other than this emphasis on how difficult it was before they arrived. This is the most significant silence in the testimonies. We know that a large number of Caribbean women lived and worked in the Canal Zone. According to the Canal Zone census of 1912, there were nearly 9,000 Jamaican men in the Canal Zone and nearly 5,000 Jamaican women. The numbers for Barbadians were just a bit lower at about 8,000 men and nearly 2,000 women. In the same year there were nearly 5,000 Caribbean children fourteen years or younger in the Canal Zone—most of whom would have been born on the Isthmus of Panama. Women (and children, to a lesser extent) played an important role, contributing to the family economy through their work in laundries, cafeterias, or as domestic servants in the white Americans' households. Yet they receive almost no mention in the Box 25 essays. As we saw in the personnel records explored in chapter 5, life partnerships between men and women were extremely important—if sometimes tense and strained.[14]

One reason why women rarely appear in the testimonies may have been the ways masculinity emerged as an important theme for canal workers, most of whom entered the zone during the early years when life and work both took place predominantly within a homosocial environment. As the comments above suggest, canal workers forced to cook, clean, and wash clothes during the early years felt discomfited by the situation. They associated the absence of women with feeling like beasts or slaves. At the same time, however, everyone sharing in these tasks generated a strong sense of alliance, brotherhood, and masculinity. The workers had to take on women's tasks even as, in their jobs, they were facing extremely arduous conditions and heavy, taxing work. Together these features likely generated a strong sense of endurance and self-reliance, which would have expressed itself as masculine values and culture. Thus, from the earliest years onward the construction project became associated with manly characteristics, and this may have encouraged the male writers in the competition to stress their autonomy and to downplay the importance of women and children in their lives.[15]

The testimonies were surprisingly silent on the Republic of Panama. The power of the United States still profoundly shaped the isthmus by the 1960s. The relationship between Panama and the United States remained a colonial one until the late twentieth century, when the Carter-Torrijos Treaty laid out the procedure for eliminating the Panama Canal Zone and granting the Republic of Panama full custody over the canal. The Canal Zone itself was effectively a colony of the United States—according to the Hay-Bunau-Varilla Treaty of 1903, the Canal Zone was the sovereign territory of the United States. And although Panama maintained formal independence, the United States gained so many powers over the republic, including the right to intervene militarily and to commandeer more territory as needed, that it became subordinated to the United States. Most of the writers in Box 25 had spent their lives working in the Canal Zone for the US government. Even as tensions over US hegemony on the isthmus rose after World War II, and the 1964 riots that would begin the process of ending US control were about to break out, as the workers sat down to write their essays in 1963, US power remained everywhere around them. So, the essays repeatedly praise and offer commentary on the US government: common refrains in the essays included statements like "the American government took care of us," or "God bless America for the God-inspired ability in building the Panama Canal." There is also one reference to how "the greater portion of people on the Isthmus hated the Americans."[16]

Even though most of the writers gave their home addresses as within the republic rather than the Canal Zone, there exist almost no references to the government of Panama in the testimonies. The few comments reflect the challenges Afro-Caribbean Panamanians faced as a result of not only the neocolonialist relationships on the isthmus but also the racism and xenophobia they faced from the people and government of Panama. Afro-Caribbeans in Panama were truly caught betwixt and between the two powers. Those who noted the role of Panama stressed the tensions in their own relationship to the Republic. For example, E. W. Martineau described the chaos that descended on the isthmus as depopulation proceeded after completion of the canal. Many people pleaded with the Panamanian government to make West Indians legal residents of the republic, he said, in recognition of their labor. Martineau praised President Belisario Porras for granting acres of land to West Indians who had helped build the canal. "This shows clearly we did not shoot our way as contrabands into the jurisdiction of the Republic, as many people has to say. We came with an olive branch . . . extending the fellowship of man to the Panamanian people although it was very difficult at the beginning to adopt ourselves to the custom and usages of the people." Martineau noted with bitterness that a Panamanian labor leader had commented that "the USA has dumped West Indians in Panama and Colón and made a great problem for us." This, said Martineau, "was not true and did not worth the paper it was written on." Like Martineau, many Afro-Caribbean Panamanians felt ostracized and underappreciated—the legacy of decades of social and political discrimination within the republic.[17]

Another writer, C. M. Weeks, noted the tense relations Afro-Caribbean Panamanians felt with Panamanians of Spanish descent, particularly in the early years. There was a sense you might be thrown in jail without even committing an infraction, he said; in part this was because you didn't know the Spanish language or Panamanian customs. Another writer expressed anger toward Panamanians. He noted the many deaths he had witnessed among West Indians during the construction era and then concluded, "That's why of today when I hear the Spaniards talk that they want the Canal, I ask them on many occasion how many Panamanians ever worked during construction days, and how many lost their lives. None of them could answer."[18]

Surviving Afro-Caribbean workers, like Constantine Parkinson, must have watched with interest in 1977 when the Carter-Torrijos Treaty passed and began the long process of granting the Republic of Panama control over the Canal Zone and the Panama Canal itself. Over time, as the racist and xenophobic laws in Panama were overturned that had made Afro-Caribbean Panamanians less than equal citizens, they came to feel some acceptance by Panamanians of Spanish descent. Yet by the end of the century discrimination against them continued to exist. While some Panamanians saw the story of the Afro-Caribbean canal diggers and dynamiters as integral to Panamanian history, others remained indifferent.

The "Colón Men" who arrived on the isthmus as teenagers and young adults moved through a world of transformation. They played a remarkable role building the Panama Canal, their experiences shaped by British and US colonialism. They faced down disease, avalanches, difficult foremen, bad food, shabby housing, torrential rainstorms, and oftentimes hostility from both Panamanians and white Zonians. How they labored under those constraints, and how they hustled to resist or accommodate themselves to the racial and gender structures around them, shaped their experiences as well. Those who labored on the canal in the decades after the construction project ended witnessed the final challenges to US power on the isthmus, the return of full sovereignty to the Republic of Panama, the demise of the most overt forms of xenophobia in the Canal Zone and in Panama, and the growing acceptance of Panamanians of Afro-Caribbean descent. Along the way, the testimonies they submitted for the Isthmian Historical Society competition ensured that their stories would be heard. Despite all the celebrating of the US government's building of the canal and the erasure of Caribbean workers' labor, these men and women gave eloquent expression to their own experiences and stories. Their descendants and the Afro-Caribbean community more generally are finding new ways to tell their stories. One hundred and ten years after the formal opening of the Panama Canal, we can still hear the voices of Box 25.

Acknowledgments

A vast community of people made the research and writing of this book possible and, indeed, enjoyable. It is fitting to begin by thanking the archivists and librarians who made this investigation of archives possible. I'm grateful to the staff at the Library of Congress, particularly Bruce Kirby, Lara Szypszak, and Patrick Kirby, who pulled Box 25 and other materials for me innumerable times. The wonderful team at the University of Florida, including John Nemmers and particularly Elizabeth "Betsy" Bemis, greatly influenced the writing of this book. Betsy Bemis was constantly creative in finding materials I didn't know existed, and in helping me understand the important work she and others are doing to collaborate with canal builder descendant communities. Staff at the National Personnel Records Center in St. Louis, Missouri; the National Archives in College Park, Maryland; the Jamaica Archives and Records Department; and the Sir Arthur Lewis Institute of Social and Economic Research at the University of the West Indies, Mona, Jamaica, also kindly supported my work. Relatedly, I am deeply grateful to Frances Williams-Yearwood and Arcelio Hartley, two descendants of canal workers who talked with me about their inspired work preserving the history of the Afro-Caribbean canal workers.

This book benefitted from a National Endowment for the Humanities Digital Grant that made possible the digitizing of hundreds of personnel files and the organizing of a workshop to explore our findings. I'm grateful to the NEH and to Caitlin Haynes, Tyler Stump, Kris Warner, and especially Jennifer Giuliano, Trevor Muñoz, and Katarina Keane for their critical assistance with this project.

Some of the ideas in this book were first discussed with scholars at a conference hosted by Oxford University, and I'm grateful to Kristin Hoganson, Jay Sexton, Julian Go, Diana Paton, Brian Delay, and many others for stimulating conversations at that time. So many historian friends have helped me think through the themes of this book, but I want especially to thank Eileen Boris, Alexander Dunphy, John Enyeart, Cindy Hahamovitch, Caitlin Kennedy, Christen Mucher, Scott Nelson, Ashley Nguyen, Kyle Pruitt, Jon Shelton, Shelton Stromquist, and Lane Windham. A very special category is made up of scholars working on Panama and Caribbean migration and who have shaped this project through their writing and conversations with me. I'm honored to be working in a field of research that includes Kaysha Corinealdi, Joan Flores-Villalobos, Jorge Giovannetti-Torres, Reena Goldthree, Marixa Lasso, Aims McGuiness, Ifeoma Nwankwo, Lara Putnam, Olive Senior, and Jacob Zumoff. I remain ever grateful to Guillermo Castro, Alfredo Castillero Calvo, and Ángeles Ramos Baquero for enhancing my understanding of Panama and its history. Panamanian filmmakers Mercedes Arias and Delfina Vidal helped me think in new ways about the testimonies in Box 25. The late Bonham Richardson generously shared his oral history research notes on Panama money in Barbados, and I will be ever grateful for that. A crucial research trip to archives in Jamaica became very productive thanks to the kind assistance and friendship of Matthew Smith and Ishtar Govia at the University of the West Indies.

I am grateful to everyone in the Department of History at the University of Maryland. For their support of my work, many thanks to Lisa Klein, Gail Russell, Jodi Hall, Wendy Bernard, and Courtney Dahlke, as well as Phil Soergel and Ahmet Karamustafa. For hallway discussions, long dinners, and coffee breaks, thanks especially to Zachary Dorner, Madeline Hsu, Clare Lyons, Quincy Mills, David Sartorius, and Colleen Woods. My dear friend, the late Ira Berlin, listened and provided feedback as I developed this project; his memory remains a blessing.

This book benefited tremendously from the ideas of my agent Lisa Adams, and I'm grateful to her for her interest and advice. My editor at The University of North Carolina Press, Debbie Gershenowitz, helped shape the book's themes and polish the writing while remaining enthusiastic in her support. I was tremendously lucky that Joan Flores-Villalobos and Jana Lipman agreed to evaluate this manuscript for the press. Their insightful suggestions truly transformed the book for the better, and my hat is off to them. For their efficient assistance with the production process, my thanks to Alexis Dumain, Iris Levesque, Elizabeth Orange, Mary C. Ribesky, Brock Schnoke, Lindsay Starr, and Varsha Venkatasubramanian.

Jim Maffie entered the world of the canal builders with me countless times, brainstorming, bouncing ideas back to me, and offering advice. I'm grateful for his wisdom and unwavering support and love. My landscape architect daughter, Sophia Florence Meinsen Maffie, possesses trustworthy instincts and a capacious knowledge of life matters big and small. Infinite thanks to them both for inspiring my life, my writing, and this book.

This book is dedicated to the memory of Constantine Parkinson, Edgar Simmons, Robert Chambers, Mary Couloote, and the many other Caribbeans who built the Panama Canal. I am grateful to all, but especially those 112 men and women who put pen to paper and gave us the powerful remembrances that became Box 25.

List of Workers with Essays in the Isthmian Historical Society Competition

CONTEST ENTRANTS

Peters, Albert; 1st prize; born Nassau, Bahamas; arrived 1906.
Martin, George H.; 2nd prize; Barbados; 1909.
Suazo, Alfonso; 3rd prize; Honduras; 1902.

Alexander, Arnold N.; ?; 1909.
Alleyne, Herbert; ?; 1908.
Allick, Helen I.; Trinidad; 1913.
Archbold, Hendrix H.; Old Providence, Colombia; 1907.
Ashby, James; ?; 1909.
Austin, Harrigan; ?; 1905.
Banister, Albert; St. Lucia; 1914?
Beckford, Reginald; Colon.
Beckles, Wesley; ?; 1913.
Belgrave, Allan C.; ?; 1905.
Berisford, G. Mitchell; Barbados; 1909.
Booth, Charles; ?; 1911.
Bowen, Samuel N.; Barbados; 1907.
Boyce, Clement C.; ?; 1909.
Bramble, Manley; ?
Brewster, Joseph; Barbados; 1906.
Brown, Lessep O.; Panama.
Brownie, Norton; ?; 1906.
Bunting, Isaiah; ?; 1910.
Burton, Eutace; ?; 1899.
Butcher, John Oswald; Barbados; 1906.
Cadogan, Samuel; ?
Carmichael, Leslie; ?; 1907.
Carr, Handel; 1911?
Chambers, Robert T.; Jamaica; 1913.
Chase, Leonard A.; ?; 1906.
Citronello, St. Justo F.; ?; 1907.
Clarke, Aaron; ?; 1906.
Clarke, Amos L.; Panama.
Clarke, Samuel; ?; 1909.
Clarke, Wesley; ?; 1911/
Clayton, H. B.; Gorgona.
Connell, James G.; Barbados; 1906.
Couloote, Mrs. Mary; St. Lucia; 1903.
Daniels, Robert S.; ?; 1906.
De la Rosa, Isaias Anticeo; ?
Doglass, Beresford; ?; 1906.
Dottin, Alfred E.; ?; 1909.
Douglas, Nehemiah E.; Jamaica; 1911.

FIGURES A.1, A.2, A.3   List of entrants to the Isthmian Historical Society Competition for the Best True Stories of Life and Work on the Isthmus of Panama, Box 25, Isthmian Historical Society, Canal Zone Library-Museum Panama Collection, Manuscript Division, Library of Congress

Finn, Enos Augustus; ?; 1905.
Forde, Rufus Edward; Trinidad; 1910.
Fox, Joseph H.; ?; 1910.
Garcia, Francisco; Panama.
Gard, Joseph H.; Barbados; 1906.
Garner, John; Barbados; 1908.
George, Augustus; ?; 1911/
Gittens, Thomas B.; Barbados; 1905.
Green, Prince George; ?; 1909?
Harnais, Bertrand Emilien; ?; 1905.
Headley, Mrs. Albertha; ?
Hermon, Peter; Barbados; 1905.
Hibbert, Isaiah N.; ?; 1911.
Hodges, George; ?; 1906.
Holder, Everton M.; ?; 1905.
Holligan, John A.; Barbados; 1906.
Hughes, Joseph Theophilus; ?; 1906.
Hunt, Clifford; ?; 1906.
Hussey, Brandt; Jamaica; 1909.
James, Frederick; Antigua; 1907.
Joseph, Jacob; Antigua; 1909.
Kavanagh, Lancelot A.; Jamaica; 1905.
Lawson, Daniel T.; Jamaica; 1906.
Leacock, Joseph; Barbados; 1906.
LeCurrieux, Jules E.; Barbados; 1906.
Lewis, James A.; Antigua; 1906.
Lucas, Rufus C.; Jamaica; 1913.
Lunche, Ange Julienne; Martinique; 1906.
McDonald, Philip; Grenada; 1908.
McEnnis, Luther; ?; 1904.
McKenzie, Z. H.; Jamaica; 1906.
Mark, John Thomas; ?; 1907.
Marshall, Joshua; ?; 1909.
Martineau, E. W.; Grenada; 1912.
Maynard, Manassah; ?; 1905.
Merchant, J. T.; ?; 1910.
Mitchell, Alfred; Jamaica; 1904.
Moore, John A.; ?; 1914.
Morgan, George W.; Jamaica; 1906.
Morgan, John; ?; 1912.
Moses, Charles; St. Lucia; 1904.
Paily, Henry; ?; 1905.
Parkinson, Constantine; Panama.
Parks, Amos; Barbados; 1914.

FIGURES A.1, A.2, A.3 (continued)

Peters, George; Dominica, B.W.I.; 1908.
Phillips, Arthur E.; ?; 1912.
Flummer, Enrique; Gorgona.
Prescod, John F.; Barbados; 1906.
Richards, John Altyman; Jamaica; 1914.
Riley, T. H.; ?; 1909.
Robinson, Samuel A.; ?
Rodrigues, Nicolas; ?
Rouse, Joseph; ?; 1905.
Ruiz, Obdulio; ?; 1910.
Sailsman, Philip Millerd; Jamaica; 1910.
St. John, Clifford; Barbados; 1905.
Sanchez, Silvero; ?; 1908.
Simmons, Edgar Llewellyn; Barbados; 1908.
Smith, Samuel A.; Jamaica; 1912.
Smith, James F.; ?; 1906.
Thomas, Charles M.; St. Lucia; 1913.
Thomas, Donald M.; ?
Thomas, Fitz H.; Barbados; 1905.
Waisome, Jeremiah; Bluefields, Nicaragua; 1895 or 1896.
Webb, Samuel; St. Vincent; 1907.
Weeks, Castilla M.; ?; 1906.
West, Alonzo F.; ?; 1912.
Wheatley, Simeon T.; ?; 1907.
White, Edward Adolphus; Jamaica; 1911.
Williams, James A.; Jamaica; 1910.

FIGURES A.1, A.2, A.3 (continued)

Notes

Introduction

1. Bonham Richardson estimates 140,000 people migrated from Jamaica and Barbados alone. Adding the smaller migratory flows from other islands of the Caribbean would easily move the numbers above 150,000. Bonham Richardson, "The Migration Experience," in *General History of the Caribbean*, ed. Bridget Brereton, Vol. V (New York: Palgrave Macmillan, 2003), 441; see also Michael Conniff, *Black Labor on a White Canal: Panama 1904-1981* (Pittsburgh, PA: University of Pittsburgh Press, 1985), chapter 2.

2. Information about the creation of the competition and the prizes awarded is from the Isthmian Historical Society Competition for the Best True Stories of Life and Work on the Isthmus of Panama, held in Box 25, Isthmian Historical Society, Canal Zone Library-Museum Panama Collection at the Library of Congress (hereafter Isthmian Historical Society competition). Although the original copies of the Box 25 testimonies are available only at the Library of Congress, a typed transcript of them held at the Afro-Antillean Museum in Panama City has recently been digitized and made available online by the University of Florida George A. Smathers Library. They can be accessed at http://ufdc.ufl.edu/AA00016037/00086/allvolumes.

3. See, for example, Rose Van Hardeveld, *Make the Dirt Fly!* (Hollywood, CA: Pan Press, 1936); William R. Scott, *The Americans in Panama* (New York: Statler, 1913); William L. Sibert and John F. Stevens, *The Construction of the Panama Canal* (New York: D. Appleton, 1915); Elizabeth Kittredge Parker, *Panama Canal Bride: A Story of the Construction Days* (New York: Exposition, 1955); Winifred James, *The Mulberry Tree* (London: Chapman and Hall, 1913); and Harry Franck, *Zone Policeman 88: A Close Range Study of the Panama Canal and Its Workers* (New York: Century, 1913).

4. Isaiah Bunting testimony, Isthmian Historical Society competition.

5. Reginald Beckford testimony, Isthmian Historical Society competition.

6. Michel-Rolph Trouillot, *Silencing the Past: Power and the Production of History* (Boston: Beacon Press, 2nd ed., 2015); Jennifer Morgan, *Reckoning with Slavery: Gender, Kinship, and Capitalism in the Early Black Atlantic* (Durham, NC: Duke University Press, 2021); Marisa J. Fuentes, *Dispossessed Lives: Enslaved Women, Violence, and the Archive* (Philadelphia: University of Pennsylvania Press, 2016); and Joan Flores-Villalobos, "'Freak Letters': Tracing Gender, Race, and Diaspora in the Panama Canal Archive," *Small Axe* 23, no. 2 (July 2019): 34–56.

7. Fuentes, *Dispossessed Lives*, 1.

8. The phrase is from Omar El Akkad's novel about the refugee crisis in Europe, *What Strange Paradise* (New York: Vintage, 2021), 201.

9. Alessandro Portelli, *The Death of Luigi Trastulli, and Other Stories: Form and Meaning in Oral History* (Albany, NY: State University of New York Press, 1991);

Daniel James, *Doña María's Story: Life History, Memory, and Political Identity* (Durham, NC: Duke University Press, 2000).

10. Jamaican Memories Collection, conducted by the *Daily Gleaner*, 1959, Jamaica Archives and Records Department, Archives Unit, Spanish Town, Jamaica; "Life in Jamaica in the Early Twentieth Century: A Presentation of Ninety Oral Accounts," Erna Brodber Oral History Project, Sir Arthur Lewis Institute of Social and Economic Research, University of the West Indies, Mona, Jamaica. See also Erna Brodber, *The Second Generation of Freemen in Jamaica, 1907-1944* (Gainesville: University of Florida Press, 2004); and Brodber, *Standing Tall: Affirmations of the Jamaican Male: 24 Self-Portraits* (Sir Arthur Lewis Institute of Social and Economic Research, University of the West Indies, Mona, Jamaica, 2003). The introduction in *Standing Tall* by George Beckford provides helpful context on the lives of the people Brodber interviewed. Bonham Richardson's interview notes in author's possession are very rich (with permission of Prof. Richardson's descendants I have shared a copy of his notes with the University of Florida archives; they will soon be available as part of the UF digital holdings). See Bonham Richardson, *Panama Money in Barbados, 1900-1920* (Knoxville: University of Tennessee Press, 1985) for his use of the interview notes. See also the oral histories collected by Pan Caribbean Sankofa and available online via the University of Florida, available at https://pcmc.uflib.ufl.edu/research/oral-histories/sankofa/sankofa-interviews/.

11. Joan Flores-Villalobos, *Silver Women: How Black Women's Labor Made the Panama Canal* (Philadelphia: University of Pennsylvania Press, 2023).

12. Useful on this theme is Lisa Yun, *The Coolie Speaks: Chinese Indentured Laborers and African Slaves in Cuba* (Philadelphia: Temple University Press, 2008).

13. Suazo and Parkinson testimonies, Isthmian Historical Society competition. The entire discussion of Parkinson and Jeremiah Waisome in these paragraphs comes from their testimonies to the Isthmian Historical Society competition.

14. On disability and prosthetic limbs in the Canal Zone see Caroline Lieffers, "Imperial Ableism: Disability and American Expansion, 1850-1930" (PhD diss., Yale University, 2020), particularly chapter 4.

Chapter One

1. Details on the US acquisition of the Panama Canal Zone can be found in John Major, *Prize Possession: The United States and the Panama Canal, 1903-1979* (Cambridge: Cambridge University Press, 1993).

2. Noel Maurer and Carlos Yu, "What T. R. Took: The Economic Impact of the Panama Canal, 1903-1937," *Journal of Economic History* 68, no. 3 (September 2008): 688, https://doi.org/10.1017/S0022050708000612. The figure of $326 million (or $10.4 billion in 2024 money) is for direct construction costs. In addition, the United States paid $10 million to Panama and $40 million to the New Panama Canal Company. Fortifications cost an additional $12 million.

3. Julie Greene, *The Canal Builders: Making America's Empire at the Panama Canal* (New York: Penguin Press, 2009), 65-70; Michael L. Conniff, *Black Labor on a White Canal: Panama, 1904-1981* (Pittsburgh, PA: University of Pittsburgh Press, 1985);

Marco Gandásegui et al., *Las Luchas Obreras En Panamá, 1850-1978*, 2nd ed. (Panama City, Panama: CELA, 1990).

4. Paul Kramer, "The Water Cure," *New Yorker*, Feb. 25, 2008; and Julie Greene, "The Wages of Empire: Capitalism, Expansionism, and Working-Class Formation," in Daniel Bender and Jana Lipman, editors, *Making the Empire Work: Labor and United States Imperialism* (New York University Press, 2015). See also Paul Kramer, *The Blood of Government: Race, Empire, the United States, and the Philippines* (Chapel Hill: University of North Carolina Press, 2006).

5. Henry Harrison Lewis, "The Panama Canal," *The Munsey*, vol. 23 (3), June 1900, 360. I am grateful to Bryan D. Palmer for sending me this article.

6. See Greene, *Canal Builders*, 200-04; *New York Times*, "Medals for Canal Diggers," Dec. 24, 1907.

7. Greene, *Canal Builders*, 205.

8. Greene, *Canal Builders*, chapter 8.

9. Marixa Lasso, *Erased: The Untold Story of the Panama Canal* (Cambridge, MA: Harvard University Press, 2019).

10. Greene, *Canal Builders*, 362.

11. Greene, *Canal Builders*, 48, 145, and note 41. References to people of African descent as "childlike" has a very long history across the Americas.

12. Frank A. Gause and Charles Carl Carr, *The Story of Panama: The New Route to India* (Boston: Silver, Burdett and Company, 1912), 134.

13. Frederic J. Haskin, *The Panama Canal* (New York: Doubleday, Page, and Co., 1913), 154; Logan Marshall, *The Story of the Panama Canal: The Wonderful Account of the Gigantic Undertaking Commenced by the French, and Brought to Triumphant Completion by the United States* (L. T. Myers, 1913).

14. Kaysha Corinealdi, *Panama in Black: Afro-Caribbean World Making in the Twentieth Century* (Durham, NC: Duke University Press, 2022), introduction; on Afro-Caribbean activism in the immediate postconstruction years see also Jacob A. Zumoff, "Black Caribbean Labor Radicalism in Panama, 1914-1921," *Journal of Social History* 47, no. 2 (Winter 2013): 429-57.

15. Corinealdi, *Panama in Black*, 4.

16. Corinealdi, *Panama in Black*, is a crucial work on this subject. On discrimination in the 1920s and 1930s, see also Jacob Zumoff, "The 1925 Tenants' Strike in Panama: West Indians, the Left, and the Labor Movement," *The Americas* 74, no. 4 (2017): 513-46; and Marixa Lasso, "Nationalism and Immigrant Labor in a Tropical Enclave: The West Indians of Colón City, 1850-1936," *Citizenship Studies* 17, no. 5 (2013): 551-65.

17. Corinealdi, *Panama in Black*, 147.

18. Corinealdi, *Panama in Black*, 147-48.

19. Corinealdi, *Panama in Black*, 149.

20. Carla Burnett, "'Are We Slaves or Free Men?' Labor, Race, Garveyism, and the 1920 Panama Canal Strike" (PhD diss., University of Illinois at Chicago, 2004), 1-27; "Cold Facts, but Warm Thoughts," *Workman*, Oct. 18, 1919; and Gerardo Maloney, *El Canal de Panamá y los trabajadores antillanos; Panamá 1920: Cronologia de una Lucha*, Ediciones Formato 16, Universidad de Panamá, 1989.

21. Corinealdi, *Panama in Black*, 80–87, 95–102; George W. Westerman, *The West Indian Worker on the Canal Zone* (Panama City: Editora Panamá América, August 1951).

22. George W. Westerman, "Blocking Them at the Canal: Failure of the Red Attempt to Control Local Workers in the Vital Panama Canal Area" (no publisher, May 1952).

23. William Jones, "Servants of Empire: Public Employee Unionism in the Panama Canal Zone, 1937–1955," unpublished paper in author's possession; Corinealdi, *Panama in Black*, 80–87, 95–102; Westerman, *West Indian Worker*.

24. Michael Donoghue, *Borderland on the Isthmus: Race, Culture, and the Struggle for the Canal Zone* (Durham, NC: Duke University Press, 2014), loc. 1351 and 1387–95.

25. Donoghue, *Borderland on the Isthmus*, chapter 2, especially loc. 1351.

26. Donoghue, *Borderland on the Isthmus*, chapter 2, loc. 1711–1814; Alan McPherson, *Yankee, No! Anti-Americanism in U.S.-Latin American Relations* (Cambridge, MA: Harvard University Press, 2003), chapter 3; Walter LaFeber, *The Panama Canal: The Crisis in Historical Perspective* (Updated ed.: New York: Oxford University Press, 1989), 135–42. On the diplomatic repercussions see Major, *Prize Possession*, 333–40.

27. Isthmian Canal Commission Records, Record Group 185, US National Archives, College Park, MD; T. B. Miskimon Papers, Special Collections, Ablah Library, Wichita State University; Foreign Office Records, National Archives, Kew, England, United Kingdom; District Courts of the United States, Records of the Panama Canal Zone, Record Group 21, US National Archives, Washington, DC.

28. Herbert and Mary Knapp, *Red, White, and Blue Paradise: The American Canal Zone in Panama* (New York: Harcourt Brace Jovanovich, 1984).

29. "What's the Question?" *Panama Canal Review*, July 5, 1963, 18–19; "The Panama Collection: A Scholarly Hallmark," *Panama Canal Review*, Feb. 1964, 10–11; on Eleanor Burnham see "Retirements," *Canal Record*, March 1967, 2.

30. On requirements for US citizens versus others, see "The Panama Canal Library, Panama Canal Zone," on the website of the Library Card Museum, https://thelibrarycardmuseum.com/2019/12/23/the-panama-canal-library/, accessed Aug. 18, 2022. For more general information about the Canal Zone Library see "Is There Anything You Want to Know? Just Ask the Staff of the C. Z. Library," *Panama Canal Review* 5, no. 2 (Sept. 3, 1954): 12.

31. *Roosevelt Medal Holders' Tape Recorder Guest Book: The Word-for-Word Reminiscences of Thirty-five Old Timers Who Helped Dig the Panama Canal*, Isthmian Historical Society, Balboa, Canal Zone, 1958 (recorded on tape Nov. 17, 1958, in connection with the Theodore Roosevelt Centennial Observations in the Canal Zone).

32. Ruth C. Stuhl and George M. Chevalier, *Isthmian Crossings: From the Collections of Ruth C. Stuhl and George M. Chevalier* (Philadelphia: Xlibris, 2001); List of Officers, Archaeological Society of Panama, *Panama Archaeologist* 5, no. 1 (December 1962): vi. I'm grateful to Elizabeth Bemis, associate curator of the Panama Canal Museum Collection, George A. Smathers Libraries, University of Florida, for helping me track down more information about Ruth Stuhl.

33. Ruth C. Stuhl, "This Was Panama," *Star and Herald*, Sept. 1962, from the Panama Canal Society website, www.pancanalsociety.org/articles/ThisWasPanama2.html.

34. Author's interview with Michele Chevalier Hagerty, the niece of Ruth Stuhl, Aug. 12, 2022.

35. Ruth Stuhl's work to preserve and catalog Panamanian history can be found in "In This Issue," *Panama Canal Review* 6 (Winter 1977); and in Box 25, Isthmian Historical Society, Canal Zone Library-Museum Panama Collection, Library of Congress, Washington, DC. I cannot confirm whether Stuhl pushed for repairing of Black as well as white gravestones, but one might guess only the latter. The disrepair of Afro-Caribbean gravestones has become a critical issue more recently in Panama, and a symbol of the continued neglect of West Indian contributions to Panamanian society. See further discussion in chapter 6.

36. Governor Fleming's comment can be found in *The Panama Canal Spillway*, Aug. 14, 1964, p. 1, University of Florida Digital Collections, https://ufdc.ufl.edu/UF00094771/00471/images.

37. Mrs. Allen M. Stuhl to *Daily Gleaner*, May 27, 1963, and attached memo, Box 25, Folder 2, Canal Zone Library-Museum Panama Collection.

38. Information on Loren B. Burnham is from *Panama Canal Spillway*, May 21, 1965, and from Box 25, Folder 2, Canal Zone Library-Museum Panama Collection. Information on Crede Calhoun comes from the *New York Times* obituary, July 7, 1978, 40. Calhoun was a collateral descendent of John C. Calhoun. Information on A. E. Osborne comes from the *Panama Canal Spillway*, July 3, 1963, and from an entry on WikiTree, www.wikitree.com/wiki/Osborne-8310, accessed Aug. 31, 2022. Osborne is notable also as being, reportedly, the second person to embrace the Baha'i faith in Panama.

39. Memo on the Isthmian Historical Society Competition for the Best True Stories of Life and Work on the Isthmus of Panama, held in Box 25, Folder 2, Isthmian Historical Society, Canal Zone Library-Museum Panama Collection, Library of Congress, Washington, DC.

40. The role of Afro-Caribbeans in Panamanian history remains a complex legacy. Many still do not feel fully integrated into or appreciated by white Panamanians, and some prefer as a result that the story of their vast diaspora not be held in Panama.

Chapter Two

1. Albert Peters submission, Isthmian Historical Society Competition for the Best True Stories of Life and Work on the Isthmus of Panama, held in Box 25, Isthmian Historical Society, Canal Zone Library-Museum Panama Collection at the Library of Congress, Washington, DC (hereafter cited as Isthmian Historical Society competition). The testimonies are also available online at the University of Florida, http://ufdc.ufl.edu/AA00016037/00001.

2. For a useful overview of sugar production across the Caribbean see Franklin Knight, "The Struggle of the British Caribbean Sugar Industry, 1900–2013," *Journal of Caribbean History* 48, no. 1/2 (2014): 149–65.

3. W. Arthur Lewis, "Foreword," in Gisela Eisner, *Jamaica, 1830–1930: A Study in Economic Growth* (Manchester, UK: Manchester University Press, 1961), xvii.

4. On the aftermath of Morant Bay see Brian L. Moore and Michele A. Johnson, *Neither Led Nor Driven: Contesting British Cultural Imperialism in Jamaica, 1865–1920* (Mona, Jamaica: University of the West Indies Press, 2004); on class structure and landholding

see Patrick Bryan, *The Jamaican People, 1880-1902: Race, Class, and Social Control* (Mona, Jamaica: University of the West Indies Press, 2012), 8–9, 132–33.

5. Bryan, *Jamaican People*, 218–27.

6. David C. Wong, "A Theory of Petty Trading: The Jamaican Higgler," *Economic Journal* 106 (March 1996), 507–18; Bryan, *Jamaican People*, 133.

7. Bonham Richardson, *Panama Money in Barbados, 1900-1920* (Knoxville: University of Tennessee Press, 2004), 53–57. On similar conditions in Antigua and St. Kitts see Robert Cassa, "The Economic Development of the Caribbean from 1880 to 1930," in *General History of the Caribbean*, Vol. V, *The Caribbean in the Twentieth Century*, ed. Bridget Brereton (New York: UNESCO and Macmillan, 2004), 10–11.

8. Henderson Carter, *Labour Pains: Resistance and Protest in Barbados, 1838-1904* (Kingston, Jamaica: Ian Randle Publishers, 2012), chap. 3, especially 165; Hilary Beckles, *Great House Rules: Landless Emancipation and Workers' Protest in Barbados, 1838-1938* (Kingston, Jamaica: Ian Randle Publishers, 2004), 125–28; Aviston D. Downes, "Barbados, 1880–1914: A Socio-Cultural History" (PhD diss., York University, 2004), 41–48; Bonham C. Richardson, "Depression Riots and the Calling of the 1897 West India Royal Commission," *New West Indian Guide* 66, no. 3/4 (1992): 169–91.

9. For an overview of Caribbean migrations see Bonham Richardson, "The Migration Experience," in *General History of the Caribbean*, ed. Bridget Brereton, Vol. V, 434–64. See also Mary Chamberlain, *Caribbean Migration: Globalised Identities* (London: Routledge, 1998); and Elizabeth Thomas-Hope, *Caribbean Migration* (Kingston, Jamaica: University of the West Indies Press, 1992).

10. Gisela Eisner, *Jamaica, 1830-1930: A Study in Economic Growth* (Manchester, UK: Manchester University Press, 1961), 147–49.

11. Eisner, *Jamaica, 1830-1930*, 150. On construction of the Panama Railroad in the mid-nineteenth century see Aims McGuinness, *Path of Empire: Panama and the California Gold Rush* (Ithaca, NY: Cornell University Press, 2009).

12. Meeting held at Mead Quarter House, Dec. 12, 1904, with canal engineer John Wallace, British consul Claude Mallet, and the governor and colonial secretary of Jamaica, Colonial Secretariat Records, Jamaica Archives and Records Department, Spanish Town, Jamaica; Julie Greene, *The Canal Builders: Making America's Empire at the Panama Canal* (New York: Penguin Press, 2009), 51; R. E. Wood to John Stevens, Oct. 22, 1906, Isthmian Canal Commission Records, Record Group 185, 2-E-1, "Labor Recruiting," US National Archives, College Park, Maryland.

13. Quoted in Downes, "Barbados, 1880–1914," 53.

14. Quoted in Richardson, *Panama Money in Barbados*, 106; from *Debates LC*, July 16, 1907, 85–87. See also Olive Senior, *Dying to Better Themselves: West Indians and the Building of the Panama Canal* (Mona, Jamaica: University of the West Indies Press, 2014), 125–26.

15. The estimates for how many Barbadians headed to Panama come from Richardson, "Migration Experience," 441. See also Downes, "Barbados, 1880–1914," 54. For the full story of Panama money's impact on Barbados, see Richardson, *Panama Money in Barbados*; the amount of remittance money comes from Hilary Beckles, *History of Barbados: From Amerindian Settlement to Nation-State* (Cambridge: Cambridge University Press, 1990), 145.

16. Notes of meetings held on Dec. 6 and Dec. 12, 1904, Colonial Secretariat Records, 1B/5/76/3/152 Emigrants Protection Law, Jamaica Archives and Records Department, Spanish Town, Jamaica. For more on these negotiations see also Senior, *Dying to Better Themselves*, 119–23.

17. Notes of meetings held on Dec. 6 and Dec. 12, 1904, Colonial Secretariat Records; Herbert G. De Lisser, *In Jamaica and Cuba* (Kingston, Jamaica: The Gleaner Co., 1910), 154–55, available online at http://ufdc.ufl.edu/UF00080939. The figure of 80,000 Jamaicans migrating to Panama is from Richardson, "Migration Experience," 441. On memories of returning Jamaicans displaying their wealth see for example the entries of Rev. R. A. L. Knight, Kingston, and H. R. Milliner, Falmouth, in the Jamaican Memories Collection, competition held by the *Jamaica Gleaner*, 1959, Jamaica Archives and Records Department, Spanish Town, Jamaica.

18. Testimonies by Harrigan Austin and Mary Couloote are in the Isthmian Historical Society competition. Information that Austin came from Barbados is in the Isthmian Canal Commission Silver Roll Personnel Records, National Personnel Records Center, St. Louis, MO. For the figure of 150,000–200,000 Caribbeans traveling to Panama, see Michael Conniff, *Black Labor on the White Canal: Panama, 1904–1981* (Pittsburgh, PA: University of Pittsburgh Press, 1985), 25–29.

19. Testimonies by Harrigan Austin, Mary Couloote, and Philip McDonald in the Isthmian Historical Society competition. See also Winifred James, *The Mulberry Tree* (London: Chapman and Hall, 1913), 190.

20. De Lisser, *In Jamaica and Cuba*, 154.

21. E. W. Martineau submission to the Isthmian Historical Society competition.

22. Daniel B. Tait, born 1874, Jamaican Memories Collection.

23. Moore and Johnson, *Neither Led Nor Driven*, 281.

24. Moore and Johnson, *Neither Led Nor Driven*, 293–97. On these questions see also Jorge L. Giovannetti-Torres, *Black British Migrants in Cuba: Race, Labor, and Empire in the Twentieth-Century Caribbean, 1898–1948* (Cambridge: Cambridge University Press, 2018), especially 118 and 236.

Chapter Three

1. This and quotations in the following paragraphs come from Harrigan Austin's testimony in the Isthmian Historical Society Competition for the Best True Stories of Life and Work on the Isthmus of Panama, held in Box 25, Isthmian Historical Society, Canal Zone Library-Museum Panama Collection at the Library of Congress, Washington, DC (hereafter cited as Isthmian Historical Society competition); information about his age, physical appearance, and parish of origin is found in his personnel records, the co-called Death Files, 185-93-0007, Box 9/182, National Personnel Records Center, St. Louis, MO.

2. For this broader history see for example Jason Colby, *The Business of Empire: United Fruit, Race, and U.S. Expansion in Central America* (Ithaca, NY: Cornell University Press, 2013); and Lara Putnam, *The Company They Kept: Migrants and the Politics of Gender in Caribbean Costa Rica, 1870–1960* (Chapel Hill: University of North Carolina Press, 2003).

3. Alfredo Castillero Calvo, *La Ruta Interoceánica y El Canal de Panamá* (Panama City, Panama: Colegio Panameño de Historiadores and Instituto del Canal de Panamá y Estudios Internacionales, 1999).

4. Joan Flores-Villalobos, *Silver Women: How Black Women's Labor Made the Panama Canal* (Philadelphia: University of Pennsylvania Press, 2023), 2–9.

5. The canal officially opened in August 1914. But in fact, dredging work to shore up the canal and repair sites affected by landslides continued for several years before the canal became fully operable. The figure of 96 million cubic yards of earth shoveled away comes from *Britannica*, www.britannica.com/topic/Panama-Canal /American-intervention.

6. Isthmian Canal Commission and H. H. Rousseau, *Census of the Canal Zone, February 1, 1912* (Mount Hope, CZ: ICC Press, 1912), 40, 47.

7. George W. Goethals, *Government of the Canal Zone* (Princeton, NJ: Princeton University Press, 1915), 2–3.

8. Marixa Lasso, *Erased: The Untold Story of the Panama Canal* (Cambridge, MA: Harvard University Press, 2019).

9. Joseph Bucklin Bishop and Farnham Bishop, *Goethals, Genius of the Panama Canal: A Biography* (New York: Harper & Brothers, 1930), 191–93; Theodore Roosevelt, *An Autobiography* (New York: Macmillan, 1913), 528; Goethals, *Government of the Canal Zone*, 50.

10. Julie Greene, *The Canal Builders: Making America's Empire at the Panama Canal* (New York: Penguin Press, 2009), 88–89.

11. Benjamin D. Weber, "The Strange Career of the Convict Clause: US Prison Imperialism in the Panamá Canal Zone," *International Labor & Working-Class History* 96 (Fall 2019): 79–102.

12. Greene, *Canal Builders*, 65–70; Michael L. Conniff, *Black Labor on a White Canal: Panama, 1904-1981* (Pittsburgh, PA: University of Pittsburgh Press, 1985); See also Marco Gandásegui et al., *Las Luchas Obreras En Panamá, 1850-1978*, 2nd ed. (Panama City, Panama: CELA, 1990).

13. According to Marc C. McLeod, for example, Cuban immigration statistics in the 1930s revealed that between 1912 and 1929, more than 90 percent of migrants from the British West Indies were able to read and write. See McLeod, "Undesirable Aliens: Race, Ethnicity, and Nationalism in the Comparison of Haitian and British West Indian Immigrant Workers in Cuba, 1912-1939," *Journal of Social History* 31, no. 3 (Spring 1998): 599–623, especially 607.

14. See also John C. Walter, "West Indian Immigrants: Those Arrogant Bastards," *Contributions in Black Studies: A Journal of African and Afro-American Studies* 5, no. 3 (Sept. 2008), https://scholarworks.umass.edu/cibs/vol5/iss1/3.

15. See Mitchell Berisford entry in the Isthmian Historical Society competition.

16. Greene, *Canal Builders*, 127–29. White skilled workers, such as blacksmiths and carpenters, were always referred to as "mechanics," while West Indians doing the same job were referred to as "artisans." The discussion above is based also on Isthmian Canal Commission personnel records, which provide a better picture of which occupations were paid monthly versus hourly.

17. Information on the labor force comes from the *Canal Record* for Sept. 22, 1909, p. 30, and Sept. 2, 1914, p. 15, University of Florida Smathers Library website, https://ufdc.ufl.edu/UF00097368/00003/42x and http://ufdc.ufl.edu/UF00097368/00029/19x. The total silver workforce for those two years was 22,449 and 27,725 respectively. The remainder of silver jobs in those two years went to salaried West Indians (which included a wide range of occupations, from white-collar employees to especially skilled craft workers, to a few relatively unskilled occupations, such as gravedigger, with unusual working hours) and European laborers.

18. John T. Hoffman et al., *The Panama Canal: An Army's Enterprise* (Washington, DC: Center of Military History, US Army, 2009), 44. See also William Gorgas, "The Conquest of the Tropics for the White Race: President's Address at the Sixtieth Annual Session of the American Medical Association, June 9, 1909," *Journal of the American Medical Association* 52, no. 25 (1909): 1967–69; Marie Cook Gorgas and Burton J. Hendrick, *William Crawford Gorgas, His Life and Work* (Garden City, NY: Doubleday, 1924). On Wallace bringing a coffin to the isthmus, see David McCullough, *The Path Between the Seas: The Creation of the Panama Canal, 1870–1914* (New York: Simon and Schuster, 1977), 447. For more information, see the recently published book by Carol R. Byerly, *Mosquito Warrior: Yellow Fever, Public Health, and the Forgotten Career of General William C. Gorgas* (Tuscaloosa: University of Alabama Press, 2024).

19. Greene, *Canal Builders*, 133.

20. William Gorgas, *Sanitation in Panama* (New York: Appleton and Co., 1916), 72; Greene, *Canal Builders*, 135–37.

21. Alfred Dottin testimony in the Isthmian Historical Society competition.

22. George Martin, Hendrix Archbold, John Holligan, Allan Belgrave, and Rufus Forde testimonies in the Isthmian Historical Society competition. Information about Belgrave's island of origin is from the Gorgas Hospital Mortuary Records, June 11, 1976, available at Ancestry.com.

23. John Prescod, Harrigan Austin, and Albert Banister testimonies in the Isthmian Historical Society competition.

24. Caetilla Weeks testimony in the Isthmian Historical Society competition.

25. Albert Peters testimony in the Isthmian Historical Society competition.

26. James Williams testimony in the Isthmian Historical Society competition.

27. Jeremiah Waisome testimony in the Isthmian Historical Society competition.

28. Amos Clarke, Edgar Simmons, and Mitchell Berisford testimonies in the Isthmian Historical Society competition.

29. Alfred Dottin, Leslie Carmichael, Clifford Hunt, and Reginald Beckford testimonies in the Isthmian Historical Society competition.

30. Amos Parks testimony in the Isthmian Historical Society competition.

Chapter Four

1. Jules LeCurrieux testimony in the Isthmian Historical Society Competition for the Best True Stories of Life and Work on the Isthmus of Panama, held in Box 25, Isthmian Historical Society, Canal Zone Library-Museum Panama Collection at the

Library of Congress, Washington, DC (hereafter cited as Isthmian Historical Society competition).

2. We explore this further in chapter 6, but for an example of Afro-Caribbean canal workers as relatively passive, see David McCullough, *The Path Between the Seas: The Creation of the Panama Canal, 1870–1914* (New York: Simon & Schuster, 1977).

3. Rhonda D. Frederick, *'Colón Man a Come': Mythographies of Panama Canal Migration* (Lanham, MD: Lexington Books, 2005), 7. Frederick's book explores the literary representations that portray Afro-Caribbean canal workers as more worldly and notes that this robust image of Black masculinity also served to erase the role of Afro-Caribbean women.

4. Had the competition drawn more submissions from people who returned home to Jamaica or Barbados, or especially those who traveled onward to New York City, the tone of impoverishment in their writings might have been diminished. In the broader African diaspora, Panama earnings helped to generate some social and economic mobility, so they may have been better off financially than those workers who remained in Panama. On this see Bonham Richardson, *Panama Money in Barbados, 1900–1920* (Knoxville: University of Tennessee Press, 2004).

5. Alonzo West, John Morgan, and Albert Banister testimonies in the Isthmian Historical Society competition.

6. George Martin, Berisford Mitchell, and Edward White testimonies in the Isthmian Historical Society competition.

7. E. W. Martineau testimony in the Isthmian Historical Society competition.

8. Enrique Plummer testimony in the Isthmian Historical Society competition.

9. Martineau and Prince George Green testimonies in the Isthmian Historical Society competition.

10. Martin testimony in the Isthmian Historical Society competition.

11. *Hearings Before the Committee on Interstate and Foreign Commerce of the House of Representatives, on the Isthmian Canal*, vol. 1 (Washington, DC: Government Printing Office, 1906), 53; John Stevens to Theodore Shonts, Dec. 14, 1905, Isthmian Canal Commission Records, 2-E-1, US National Archives and Records Administration, College Park, MD.

12. Rufus Lucas, Jules E. LeCurrieux, and Constantine Parkinson testimonies in the Isthmian Historical Society competition.

13. Martineau, Jeremiah Waisome, and Harrigan Austin testimonies in the Isthmian Historical Society competition.

14. Eric Walrond quotation is from his story "Panama Gold" in *Tropic Death* (New York: Collier Books, 1954), 103; quoted also in James Davis, *Eric Walrond: A Life in the Harlem Renaissance and the Transatlantic Caribbean* (New York: Columbia University Press, 2015), 119.

15. Julie Greene, *The Canal Builders: Making America's Empire at the Panama Canal* (New York: Penguin Press, 2009), 146–47.

16. For more on this see Greene, *Canal Builders*, chapter 3.

17. The silver and gold payroll system became central to the US effort to segregate and discipline its workforce. For more on this aspect of US labor management, see Greene, *Canal Builders*; Olive Senior, *Dying to Better Themselves: West Indians and*

the Building of the Panama Canal (Mona, Jamaica: University of the West Indies Press, 2014); and Michael Conniff, *Black Labor on the White Canal: Panama, 1904–1981* (Pittsburgh, PA: University of Pittsburgh Press, 1985).

18. Alfonso Suazo testimony in the Isthmian Historical Society competition.

19. The work of T. B. Miskimon, Goethals's inspector, can be traced by examining his personal papers. To cite just one example, see T. B. Miskimon to Goethals, April 25, 1907, Folder 1, T. B. Miskimon Papers, Special Collections, Ablah Library, Wichita State University, MS 86-5.

20. Mallet's role is seen in correspondence in the Foreign Office Records of the UK National Archives. For background information on Mallet see Matthew Parker, *Panama Fever: The Epic Story of the Building of the Panama Canal* (New York: Anchor Books, 2007).

21. Claude Mallet to Consul Cox, Dec. 8, 1910, Foreign Office 371/944, UK National Archives.

22. Claude Mallet to Governor Magoon, Jan. 17, 1906, Foreign Office 371/101; and Claude Mallet to Sir, Nov. 19, 1906, Foreign Office 288/98. For a more positive perspective on Mallet's career, see Parker, *Panama Fever*.

23. J. Keir Hardie to Colonel Seely, Colonial Office, Nov. 24, 1908, Foreign Office 271/494; see also the handwritten note on Mallet's letter to Sir, Nov. 19, 1906, Foreign Office 288/98.

24. No author to Mallet, Sept. 26, 1914, Foreign Office 288/160; Jacob Marsh to the Foreign Secretary of State, United Kingdom, Jan. 7, 1911, Foreign Office 371/1176. For other examples of Caribbean workers appealing to their rights as British subjects, see Greene, *Canal Builders*, e.g., 264; and Jorge Giovannetti-Torres, *Black British Migrants in Cuba: Race, Labor, and Empire in the Twentieth-Century Caribbean, 1898–1948* (New York: Cambridge University Press, 2018), 236.

25. Claude Mallet to Sir Edward Grey, May 6, 1910; H. O. Chalkley, Vice-Consul, to C. C. Mallet, May 3, 1910; and A. Innes to Grey, Oct. 21, 1910; all Foreign Office 371/943.

26. William J. Karner, *More Recollections* (Boston: T. Todd, 1921), 41.

27. Walrond, "Panama Gold," 42. Discussed also in Davis, *Eric Walrond*, 120.

28. See Reena Goldthree, "'A Greater Enterprise than the Panama Canal': Migrant Labor and Military Recruitment in the World War I-Era Circum-Caribbean," in *Labor: Studies in Working-Class History of the Americas*, ed. Julie Greene and Leon Fink, 57–82, especially 58–59.

29. On the number of workers employed during the construction decade see Conniff, *Black Labor*; on the vast project to dismantle historic towns of Panama as construction of the canal wrapped up, see Marixa Lasso, *Erased: The Untold Story of the Panama Canal* (Cambridge, MA: Harvard University Press, 2019).

Chapter Five

1. Information on the size and holdings of the National Personnel Records Center (hereafter NPRC), St. Louis, MO, comes from the website of the National Archives, www.archives.gov/press/press-kits/nprc-st-louis/facts-and-figures.html.

2. Since 2016, when I last conducted research at the NPRC to find more information about the writers in Box 25, Family Search, a corporation, has digitized many documents related to silver and gold workers in the Canal Zone. As a result one can now search their online holdings for more information as well. However, the NPRC continues to hold vastly more information than is available via Family Search. Family Search digitized only two or three document types: Metal Check Issue Cards from 1937, the Application for Photo-Metal Checks from 1918, and Service Record Cards. Each type of document provides useful information but only a snapshot of a worker's life from one moment in time. At the NPRC, by contrast, it is possible to access the entire personnel file for many individuals, providing information on their work lives over several decades.

3. This is because much of the material held at the NPRC has not yet been processed and so is not available to researchers. In general, the files that have been processed belong to workers who continued working on the Panama Canal for many years.

4. Marixa Lasso, *Erased: The Untold Story of the Panama Canal* (Cambridge, MA: Harvard University Press, 2019); Michael Conniff, "Black Labor on the White Canal: West Indians in Panama, 1904–1980" (working paper, University of New Mexico, Albuquerque, 1983), https://digitalrepository.unm.edu/ laii_research/17.

5. Statistics on the West Indian population in the Canal Zone and Republic of Panama are from Michael Conniff, *Black Labor on the White Canal: Panama, 1904–1981* (Pittsburgh, PA: University of Pittsburgh Press, 1985), 63 and 66.

6. Personnel Record for Leon Pierre Marie Coquelin, Panama Canal Commission Death Files, Box 40, 185-93-0007, NPRC. See also, for example, the Death Files on Harold King, Box 90; and Jonathan Francis, Box 58.

7. As discussed in chapter 4, because Jamaicans had to pay an emigration tax to leave the island, and the fact that a larger independent peasantry and Black middle class existed there, those in the Canal Zone were likely to work at more skilled jobs.

8. Christopher Corbin's case comes from the Panama Canal Commission Death Files, Box 40, 185-93-0007, particularly the Personnel Record of Silver Employee, Nov. 25, 1938.

9. Robert Chambers, Panama Canal Commission Death Files, 185-93-0007, 32/172, 13 LC Row 17.

10. Harrigan Austin, Death Files, 185-93-0007, Box 9/182. A search for Lillian Austin in the digitized records of Family Search finds her living in New York City in 1940 and in 1950, according to the US census for those years: www.familysearch.org/ark:/61903 /1:1:K316-PT5.

11. Information here and in preceding paragraphs comes from Constantine Parkinson, Death Files, 85-93-0007, Box 120/172. Parkinson's plea to Goethals is dated July 27, 1914.

12. John J. Claybourn, Memorandum for the Executive Secretary, July 13, 1931; internal memo on S. A. Smith, n.d.; C. A. M. [McIlvaine], Memorandum for Mr. Lombard, June 30, 1931; C. A. McIlvaine, Executive Secretary, to S. A. Smith, July 3 and 8, 1931; all Samuel Smith Death Files, 185-93-0007, Box 149/172, 13 LC Row 16.

13. Joan Flores-Villalobos, *The Silver Women: How Black Women's Labor Made the Panama Canal* (Philadelphia: University of Pennsylvania Press, 2023), 33–36, 80–82.

14. Edith Blake to Paul Wilson, June 27, 1931; S. A. Smith to Dear Sir, July 1, 1931; Edith Blake to Samuel Smith, Dec. 13, 1931; Samuel Smith to Dear Sir, Jan. 21, 1932; C. A. McIlvaine to Acting Superintendent, Dredging Division, May 25, 1933; all Smith Death Files.

15. On Obeah see Diana Paton, "The Racist History of Jamaica's Obeah Laws," July 4, 2019, *History Workshop Journal*, www.historyworkshop.org.uk/empire-decolonisation/the-racist-history-of-jamaicas-obeah-laws/, accessed Jan. 21, 2024; and Diana Paton, *The Cultural Politics of Obeah: Religion, Colonialism, and Modernity in the Caribbean World* (New York: Cambridge University Press, 2015).

16. Edith Blake to My Dear Respectful Gentleman, Oct. 22, 1934; S. A. Smith to C. A. McIlvaine, Dec. 19, 1934; Edith Blake to Executive Secretary, Jan. 3, 1935; P. A. White to John G. Claybourn, Jan. 9, 1935; all Smith Death Files.

17. C. A. S. to Mr. Paul, January 1931, Smith Death Files.

18. Samuel Smith to J. G. Claybourn, Aug. 13, 1938; S. A. S. to Mr. Paul, Sept. 7, 1938; Seymour Paul to Superintendent, Dredging Division, Sept. 13, 1938; all Smith Death Files.

19. Seymour Paul to Samuel Smith, May 8, 1940; Seymour Paul to Edith Blake, April 22, 1940, Smith Death Files.

20. Personnel Record for Samuel Smith, Smith Death Files.

21. Disability Relief Board Summary for Samuel A. Smith, Mar. 13, 1956, Smith Death Files; Samuel A. Smith, Isthmian Historical Society Competition for the Best True Stories of Life and Work on the Isthmus of Panama, held in Box 25, Isthmian Historical Society, Canal Zone Library-Museum Panama Collection at the Library of Congress, Washington, DC.

22. Emma Boyce to Executive Secretary, Oct. 11, 1938; Seymour Paul, Memo for General Manager, Commissary Division, Oct. 13, 1938; Clement Boyce to Dear Sir, Oct. 16, 1938; Seymour Paul to Emma Boyce, Oct. 30, 1938; all Smith Death Files.

23. For more on marriage and divorce among West Indians see Flores-Villalobos, *Silver Women*, especially 96–109; and Olive Senior, *Dying to Better Themselves: West Indians and the Building of the Panama Canal* (Kingston, Jamaica: University of the West Indies Press, 2014), 245–50.

Chapter Six

1. Jules LeCurrieux testimony in the Isthmian Historical Society Competition for the Best True Stories of Life and Work on the Isthmus of Panama, held in Box 25, Isthmian Historical Society, Canal Zone Library-Museum Panama Collection at the Library of Congress, Washington, DC (hereafter cited as Isthmian Historical Society competition.

2. Michel-Rolph Trouillot, *Silencing the Past: Power and the Production of History*, 2nd rev. ed. (Boston: Beacon Press, 2015), chapter 1, especially Loc. 546.

3. Willis J. Abbot, *Panama and the Canal in Picture and Prose: A Complete Story of Panama, as Well as the History, Purpose and Promise of Its World-Famous Canal* (London: Syndicate Pub, 1913), 19, 22.

4. Farnham Bishop, *Panama Past and Present* (New York: The Century Co., 1916), 203.

5. J. Saxon Mills, *The Panama Canal: A History and Description of the Enterprise* (London: T. Nelson and Sons, 1913), 165–66.

6. Winifred James, *The Mulberry Tree* (London: G. Bell and Sons, 1913), 39–40.

7. James, *Mulberry Tree*, 139.

8. James, *Mulberry Tree*, 40, 45–46.

9. Joseph Bucklin Bishop, *The Panama Gateway* (New York: Charles Scribner's Sons, 1913), 315, 300. On this see also Bishop, *Panama Past and Present*, 203.

10. William J. Karner, *More Recollections* (Boston: T. Todd, 1921), 41–42.

11. Gerstle Mack, *The Land Divided: A History of the Panama Canal and Other Isthmian Canal Projects* (New York: Knopf, 1944), 538, 541.

12. David McCullough, *The Path Between the Seas: The Creation of the Panama Canal, 1870-1914* (New York: Simon & Schuster, 1977).

13. McCullough, *Path Between the Seas*, 574–79.

14. McCullough, *Path Between the Seas*, 580. The comment was made by D. T. Lawson, testimony in the Isthmian Historical Society competition, Box 25, Isthmian Historical Society, Canal Zone Library-Museum Panama Collection, Library of Congress, Washington, DC.

15. McCullough, *Path Between the Seas*, 581–85.

16. Matthew Parker, *Panama Fever: The Epic Story of the Building of the Panama Canal* (New York: Anchor Books, 2007), 437–38.

17. Michael Conniff, *Black Labor on a White Canal: Panama, 1904-1981* (Pittsburgh, PA: University of Pittsburgh Press, 1985).

18. Lancelot S. Lewis, *The West Indian in Panama: Black Labor in Panama, 1850-1914* (Washington, DC: University Press of America, 1980); on Lewis's view of Black laborers in the zone as passive see Jacob A. Zumoff, "Black Caribbean Labor Radicalism in Panama, 1914-1921," *Journal of Social History* 47, no. 2 (Winter 2013): 429–57, particularly 433.

19. George W. Westerman, *Los Immigrantes Antillanos en Panamá* (Panama: Editorial Biblioteca Nacional, 2018 [1980]); Velma Newton, *The Silver Men: West Indian Labour Migration to Panama 1850-1914* (Kingston, Panama: Ian Randle, 1984). For an even earlier—and influential—exploration see George W. Westerman, "Historical Notes on West Indians on the Isthmus of Panama," *Phylon* 22, no. 4 (1961): 340–50. A Panamanian study that makes limited use of the testimonies in Box 25 (actually just quoting passages from Lancelot Lewis's work) is Gerardo Maloney, *El Canal de Panamá y los trabajadores antillanos; Panamá 1920: Cronologia de una Lucha* (Panama City, Panama: Ediciones Formato 16, Universidad de Panamá, 1989), e.g., 13–14.

20. Olive Senior, *Dying to Better Themselves: West Indians and the Building of the Panama Canal* (Kingston, Jamaica: University of the West Indies Press, 2014), xviii.

21. Senior, *Dying to Better Themselves*, xix.

22. Senior, *Dying to Better Themselves*, 9.

23. Senior, *Dying to Better Themselves*, 111.

24. Joan Flores-Villalobos, *The Silver Women: How Black Women's Labor Made the Panama Canal* (Philadelphia: Penn Press, 2022), 41–42, 143, 51.

25. All information and quotations in these paragraphs come from Roman Foster, comments made during Memory Lane: Exploring the Lives of Caribbean People at the

Panama Canal in the 20th Century, a community event hosted by Pan-Caribbean Sankofa and the Panama Canal Museum Collection at the University of Florida, Sept. 3–14, 2022, video link shared by Elizabeth Bemis with the author (it will later be available online at the UF library website).

26. *Box 25: The Untold Story of the Panama Canal*, documentary film produced and directed by Delfina Vidal and Mercedes Arias (Panama City, Panama: Adler and Associates Entertainment, 2015). The author served as a historical consultant on the film.

27. Author's discussion with Frances Williams-Yearwood, Feb. 23, 2024.

28. The quotation is from the Cemetery Preservation Foundation website at www.cgmcemeteryfoundation.org/what-we-do.

29. The quotation on the mission of the Panama Canal Society is available at its website, https://pancanalsociety.org/.

30. For more information on PanCaribbean Sankofa visit www.cgmcemeteryfoundation.org/pan-caribbean-sankofa. The oral histories created by PCS are available at https://pcmc.uflib.ufl.edu/research/oral-histories/sankofa/sankofa-interviews/.

31. Author's discussion with Williams-Yearwood; author's discussion with Elizabeth Bemis, Jan. 2, 2024. For more information on the Afro-Antillean Museum in Panama City, which is maintained by the Society of Friends of the West Indian Museum of Panama, visit https://samaap.com/.

32. Author's discussion with Williams-Yearwood.

33. Marguerite Vargas-Betancourt, "Finding the Silver Voice: Afro-Antilleans in the Panama Canal Museum Collection at the University of Florida," unpublished conference presentation, 2013, available at https://ufdc.ufl.edu/IR00003593/00001/pdf.

34. The Silver La Boca Project is available at https://pcmc.uflib.ufl.edu/laboca/.

35. Elizabeth Bemis's comment was made during a Memory Lane session, Sept. 14, 2022, www.youtube.com/watch?v=onSENpGb6Lc&ab_channel=PanCaribbean Sankofa.

36. Author's discussion via Zoom with Arcelio Hartley, Mar. 2, 2024. Information in the following paragraphs is also from this discussion. On discrimination in Panama towards people of African descent in recent decades, see also George Priestley and Alberto Barrow, "The Black Movement in Panama: A Historical and Political Interpretation, 1994–2004," *Souls: A Critical Journal of Black Politics, Culture, and Society* 10 (2008): 232–33; and George Priestley, "Post-Invasion Panama: Urban Crisis and Social Protest," in *Globalization and Survival in the Black Diaspora: The New Urban Challenge*, ed. Charles St. Clair Green (New York: State University of New York Press, 1997), 85–107.

Conclusion

1. Constantine Parkinson to Ronald L. Seeley, Personnel Director, PCC, June 16, 1983, and Sept. 19, 1985, Box 120, Constantine Parkinson Death Files, National Personnel Records Center, St. Louis, MO.

2. Lilia Knotts to Manager, Chase Manhattan Bank, July 14, 1987, Report of Death of Disability Relief Recipient, Dec. 31, 1989, Box 120, Constantine Parkinson Death Files.

3. "C. Parkinson P.C. Retiree," *Star and Herald*, Dec. 5, 1957, Box 120, Constantine Parkinson Death Files.

4. A. H. McKenzie and Samuel A. Smith testimonies in the Isthmian Historical Society Competition for the Best True Stories of Life and Work on the Isthmus of Panama, held in Box 25, Isthmian Historical Society, Canal Zone Library-Museum Panama Collection at the Library of Congress, Washington, DC (hereafter cited as Isthmian Historical Society competition).

5. Michel-Rolph Trouillot, *Silencing the Past: Power and the Production of History*, 2nd ed. (Boston: Beacon Press, 2015), chapter 1, Loc. 502.

6. Samuel Smith, Jeremiah Waisome, and Amos Clarke (on the first airplane) testimonies in the Isthmian Historical Society competition.

7. Caetilla Weeks and Amos Parks testimonies in the Isthmian Historical Society competition. See also George W. Westerman, "Historical Notes on West Indians on the Isthmus of Panama," *Phylon* 22, no. 4 (1961): 342–43. According to Westerman there were thirteen Anglican congregations in the zone during early construction days.

8. Waisome testimony in the Isthmian Historical Society competition.

9. Clifford Hunt testimony in the Isthmian Historical Society competition.

10. On money, see Constantine Parkinson and Philip McDonald testimonies in the Isthmian Historical Society competition.

11. Albert Banister testimony in the Isthmian Historical Society competition.

12. Joseph H. Fox, John Butcher, and Jules E. LeCurrieux testimonies in the Isthmian Historical Society competition.

13. Alfred Dottin, Jules LeCurrieux, Philip McDonald, and Harrigan Austin testimonies in the Isthmian Historical Society competition. The importation of Martinican women to which Harrigan Austin refers generated a major scandal for the US government, as charges were made that the United States was providing prostitutes to the men. On this see Julie Greene, *The Canal Builders: Making America's Empire at the Panama Canal* (New York: Penguin Press, 2009); and Joan Flores-Villalobos, *The Silver Women: How Black Women's Labor Made the Panama Canal* (Philadelphia: University of Pennsylvania Press, 2023).

14. *Census of the Canal Zone*, Feb. 1, 1912 (Mount Hope, CZ: ICC Press, 1912), 29–31. On Caribbean women's important role in the construction project see Flores-Villalobos, *Silver Women*.

15. The classic work on homosocial environments and masculinity is Susan Lee Johnson, *Roaring Camp: The Social World of the California Gold Rush* (New York: W. W. Norton & Company, 2000); see also Madeline Y. Hsu, "Unwrapping Orientalist Constraints: Restoring Homosocial Normativity to Chinese American History," *Amerasia Journal* 29, no. 2 (2003): 230–53.

16. E. W. Martineau, James Lewis, and T. H. Riley testimonies in the Isthmian Historical Society competition.

17. Martineau testimony in the Isthmian Historical Society competition.

18. Weeks and Parks testimonies in the Isthmian Historical Society competition.

Index

Canal Zone. *See* Panama Canal Zone